PRAISE FOR

Reconfigured

"Stirringly inspirational. . . . The memoir's power is in its message that suffering 'carves out space' in our hearts 'for more compassion,' and illness provides an opportunity for us to discover our better selves."

—*Kirkus Reviews*

"Barbara has written a beautiful account of her journey with marriage, motherhood, cancer, and finding her own place in the world. Those familiar with Whidbey will appreciate the lovely sketches of life on our beloved island. Those who have sustained or hope to sustain long-term relationships will be grateful for the honesty about what they entail."

—MICHAEL LERNER, president and cofounder of Commonweal and cofounder of Healing Circles Langley, Healing Circles Global, cancerchoices.org, and Commonweal Cancer Help Program

"I greatly appreciate Barbara's transformative memoir written with honesty, vulnerability, and courage. She faced life challenges of cancer, marriage issues, and relocation with grit and grace. Her Buddhist perspective reminds me of the analogy of the lotus flower. Out of adversity she reclaimed her authentic Self."

—SUSAN WISEHART, MS, LMFT, holistic psychotherapist and author of *Soul Visioning: Clear the Past, Create Your Future*

"*Reconfigured* is a deeply moving and absorbing chronicle of Barbara Wolf Terao's cancer journey, but, even more, of her path toward wholeness, home, and her authentic self. This beautifully written book reminds us all to listen to and trust not just ourselves but also the universe."

—DONNA CAMERON, author of *A Year of Living Kindly: Choices That Will Change Your Life and the World Around You*

"Barbara is one terrific writer! What I find remarkable is her way of interweaving 'things spiritual' with nitty-gritty aspects of dealing with cancer. She gave voice to much of what I felt going through my own cancer experiences."

—BRADFORD GARTON,
composer and professor of music at Columbia University

"A compelling story, filled with spirit! As a breast cancer survivor, I received guidance, affirmation, and inspiration from this book. The ways Barbara copes with her reconfiguration can benefit anyone going through changes."

—KATHLEEN HUDSON, PHD,
poet, author, and professor of English at Schreiner University

"In her memoir of seeking and finding, Barbara Wolf Terao invites readers into her circle of friends, family members, doctors, nurses, ferryboat personnel, and shoe salesmen. It's a big, beautiful circle on Whidbey Island, and one I did not want to leave. . . . She approaches all her challenges with wit, grit, and a belief in nature and spirit that inspires and warms."

—SHARON FIFFER, author of *Imagining America* and the Jane Wheel mysteries and coeditor of *Home: American Writers Remember Rooms of Their Own, Family: American Writers Remember Their Own*, and *Body*

"To read *Reconfigured* is to be transported via the unlikely vehicles of a troubled marriage, a cancer diagnosis, and an enchanted desert horse to a place of understanding of what it means to be alive. Changing her karma with every challenge, Barbara literally turns her medications from poison to medicine and figuratively does the same with her new life on Whidbey Island. I couldn't help but cheer her on her way!"

—NANCY SLONIM ARONIE, founder of the Chilmark Writing Workshop and author of *Memoir as Medicine* and *Writing from the Heart: Tapping the Power of Your Inner Voice*

Reconfigured

A Memoir

Barbara Wolf Terao

SHE WRITES PRESS

Published 2023
Printed in the United States of America
Print ISBN: 978-1-64742-499-2
E-ISBN: 978-1-64742-502-9
Library of Congress Control Number: 2022917724

For information, address:
She Writes Press
1569 Solano Ave #546
Berkeley, CA 94707

Book Design by Stacey Aaronson

She Writes Press is a division of SparkPoint Studio, LLC.

To all the book lovers in my family, especially my mom and dad,
Joy and Frank Wolf.

"Will we let the wind sing to us? Do our whole bodies listen?
When the wind calls, will we go?"

—SUSAN GRIFFIN

TABLE OF CONTENTS

MY RIDE IS HERE

*W*ho goes looking for cancer on the unlucky day of Friday the thirteenth of December? I did when I ended up at a Seattle medical center to sample abnormal tissue identified by my mammogram in Illinois three weeks earlier.

Around 10 percent of Americans say they avoid thirteens. In tarot and numerology, thirteen is considered spooky by some because it can signify death.

Since I moved from Illinois to Washington state, those digits pointed their bony fingers at me wherever I went. For instance, at a writers' workshop, I was thirteenth in line to read my essay to the group. My monthly health insurance premium was four figures plus thirteen cents. One of the hospitals I had to go to was on 13th Street. The other was reached via Exit 13. Even the lot I chose for a house on Whidbey Island was number thirteen. Maybe that's why it was still available.

I remembered the application I'd filled out for compensation for my father's death related to his work as a radiation monitor during nuclear bomb testing on Bikini Atoll in the Marshall Islands. Of the compensable diseases listed by the US Radiation Exposure Compensation Act, my father's type of lung cancer was number thirteen. Dad was a mathematician, so I sometimes noticed numbers that made me think of him. By chance, I often looked at the clock at 3:33 p.m., which was the time I heard of my dad's death on July 1, 2000, and it is just a cool number. The decimal number for one-third consists of threes repeating forever, which I like to think is a sign of my father's ongoing presence. Was the number thirteen appearing as a warning from Dad of what to expect from my biopsy?

And what was up with the black cats? Why were they suddenly strolling in front of me on a much-too-frequent basis? Two crossed my path in one day as I walked around the seaside town of Coupeville on Whidbey Island. The old story from Europe was that black cats were bad luck because they were witches in disguise. Already worried about cancer due to my suspicious mammogram results, I wondered if the numbers and cats were indicative of my imminent demise.

Of the annual average of six hundred thousand deaths in the United States from cancer reported by the National Cancer Institute, more than forty thousand of them are due to invasive breast cancer. An Illinois friend, much younger than me, had been diagnosed with breast cancer and died within months. Would I soon be part of those statistics?

Then, parked on a charming Coupeville street, I saw a white hearse—with my name on it, of all things. On its side, in pink, were the words, "Barbie's Dream Hearse." The dark-haired owner, Kat (in keeping with the feline theme of the day), told me she decorated the old car like Barbie's dream house and drove it for hire. Having the name Barbara, I had often been called Barbie. Was this brazen omen the final nail in my coffin?

My ride is here, I thought, not sure whether to be amused or horrified. To be reminded of a toy dominated by her breasts at a time when I faced the prospect of losing mine was bizarre. Well, at least this death cab was dolled up for the journey and provided levity at a time when an ominous kind of gravity weighed me down. While not denying the gravitas of my situation, I liked to think I'd be going in style—the cute style of a doll created in the 1950s around the same time I was.

❀

While back in the Chicago area for Thanksgiving, I'd used my Illinois insurance one last time before switching to health care coverage in my new state of Washington. I had my routine mammogram. Four days later, I was called back for a magnified mammogram and ultrasound; tumors were found in my right breast. Upon my return to Whidbey Island, my new home, I'd been scrambling to set up a time to investigate those tumors and the insurance to cover it. Despite the dismal date of Friday the thirteenth, I was glad to get the appointment and ready to have my tests done.

I was also glad to have a friend, Carla, accompany me on this, my first visit to my health maintenance organization's oncology department. Though Carla was a new friend, one of the first I made on Whidbey Island, she became a source of support. Her help was especially appreciated when my husband, Donald, was away in Illinois, which was most of the time. (My daughter, Emily, lived nearby but was busy working long hours.)

When I told Carla I faced the prospect of cancer and wasn't sure where the journey would take me, she simply said, "I'm going with you." Her husband had died of cancer, which was devastating to her, and yet she did not hesitate to enter that perilous terrain again, with me. Carla and I shared a similar optimistic outlook on life. She helped me keep hope alive. One good friend can dispel any number of bad omens.

The spacious waiting room had views of the snow-capped Cascade Mountains to the east and was empty except for us. I imagined wiser patients filling the chairs on previous luckier days. Carla and I settled in for a wait, which wasn't long. But the appointment got off to a bad start. The medical assistant, Portia, called me in, sat me down, and told me I'd be getting tissue samples taken from my left breast.

"Left?" I asked.

She confirmed, showing me the paperwork designating that side of my body.

This was not reassuring. The hospital paperwork was wrong. I never felt so much as a twinge from the tumors, but I knew where they were located. The words of the radiologist who told me the results of my magnified mammogram and ultrasound back in Illinois in November still rang in my head. "It looks like you have tumors in your right breast," she said, her eyes boring into mine with an intensity that commanded my full attention. "You need to get biopsies of those right away."

When I told Portia this, she had Dr. Reed, the radiologist doing the biopsy procedure, straighten out the confusion. We finally all agreed there was no problem identified with my left breast. It was my right side that had tumors needing testing.

For the procedure, the nurse applied lidocaine to numb the area. I was then raised on a wooden platform, like a tree house of torture, almost to the ceiling, lying on my stomach, with my right breast poking through a hole for the stereotactic biopsies. Seven of the samplings only required some calm breathing to endure. But one needle punch was intensely painful, and I said so. My hands and arms started to tingle, and I felt faint and nauseous. Portia stepped up on a stool and came to my aid with a cool, damp cloth for my head. As I recovered, Dr. Reed finished his needling.

On my way out, Portia offered me a soothing ice pack for my sore breast. I asked for a second one for the road. I wanted more of anything that gave me support. If the biopsies showed cancer, I was in for a long, hard journey. I wanted to bring Portia and her cool, soft towel home with me till this whole thing was over. I held the cold comfort of the ice pack to my chest, and Carla drove me back to the island.

Four days later, I was in my Langley house, keeping myself occupied by wrapping Christmas gifts, unpacking boxes I'd sent myself from Illinois, and researching cancer. I tried not to obsess over my health, though I was anxious to hear the results. If there was cancer in me, I wanted it removed as soon as possible.

Internet service was not yet hooked up to my house, so I used my cell phone for all my online activities. On that Tuesday, I sat at my dining room table, scrolling through social media. I paused on a black-and-white photograph that caught my eye. My cousin, Rick, had posted a picture of our grandmother, Helen Wolf, in her Webster Groves home. I was named Barbara Helen Wolf with her in mind, and I was particularly fond of her. In the old photo, my white-haired grandmother had a soft smile on her face and held a grandchild, my cousin Kerry.

Just then my cell phone chimed, and the photo disappeared as I answered the call. It was a nurse calling from my HMO with my diagnosis: invasive ductal carcinoma.

"It is HER/2 positive," she said, "which means it's an aggressive type of breast cancer. It is also estrogen positive, which gives you some treatment options." I went into information-gathering mode and asked her some questions. Terror buzzed in the back of my mind like a chainsaw, but acknowledging my emotions would come later, after I sorted through the facts. I tend to compartmentalize when faced with alarming or excruciating situations. When I understood what I had to do next, such as setting up appointments with an oncologist and a surgeon, we ended the call.

It was then that my grandmother came back into view on my cell phone. Gazing at her, dazed from the impact of my diagnosis, I suddenly realized, *Oh! She had terminal breast cancer when she was seventy-nine. She's here to keep me company at this difficult time.* Whether her appearance was a coincidence or not, it was a huge comfort, like a hug from a loved one, even if it came from beyond the grave.

"Thank you for being with me, Grandmom," I told her with tears in my eyes. Then I had to ask, "Was it you who nudged me to get my mammogram? By catching it earlier than you did, maybe I have a chance."

....

2

CONFLUENCES

*I think when Minnesotans talk obsessively about the weather
we are trying, in our peculiarly reticent way, to describe the
passionate uncertainty of our carefully concealed lives.*
—JOAN PREFONTAINE

y hometown smells like breakfast. When the Malt-O-Meal Company makes their hot cereal, the aroma of malted grains wafts from Ames Mill, across the Cannon River, and into the shopping district of Northfield, Minnesota. Once the homeland of the Wahpekute Band of the Dakota people, Northfield became a mill town named after settler John Wesley North. According to the welcome sign near St. Olaf College, it is now a city of cows, colleges, and contentment. Residents have pride in local history, holding an annual celebration of the 1876 defeat of the notorious Jesse James gang.

As I was growing up, we welcomed the gentle fragrance of Malt-O-Meal as part of our image of contentment. However, nobody wanted to talk about the cola-colored Cannon River, polluted by industrial and agricultural runoff, flowing through town. Reality was overlooked for the sake of appearances—and commerce.

As much as I liked living among the people and prairies of

Minnesota, I felt like a misfit. I never got the hang of the rural reticence, Protestant piety, or football fanaticism. Had I landed on the wrong planet? It wasn't until I saw the 1996 movie *Fargo* that I realized how immersed I was in the culture of Midwestern Nice, which is the practice of keeping up appearances and saying only what is necessary—or maybe even less than that.

I appreciated courteous behavior and knew that if I stood on a street corner in Minneapolis looking lost, someone would likely offer help before I even asked for it. Yet the friendliness was combined with a chilly reserve that confused me. Describing local culture, former Minneapolis Mayor R.T. Rybak said, "Minnesotans will give you directions to anywhere but their house."

What mattered to me was rarely addressed. I ached to talk about feelings, fears, and personal philosophies as I made sense of my own experiences. And I wanted to get to know people through such discussions. In Northfield, I felt foolish for trying. Still, I tuned into subtle body language, eyebrow movements, and tone of voice to squeeze more meaning out of the coded communication of the Germanic and Nordic people of my family and community. I kept my antennae tuned to those messages, spoken and unspoken, trying to get along in the place where I'd landed.

St. Olaf professor, Kari LieDorer, explained to a journalist that Scandinavian social norms require humility to the point of self-erasure, with indirect communication often indistinguishable from passive aggression. Those were not norms I cared to adopt. I wanted to find a place safe enough to be me. It would take me decades to do so.

My father, Frank, was a math professor and usually had summers off (or could work from home writing textbooks), so we'd go north to the home we called Old Orchard on Bay Lake. Before my mother, Joy, started her career as a librarian, she was free to go north too. During the four-hour drive, I sat in the back seat of our Chevrolet station wagon with my two sisters and our Brittany spaniel, Princess. Eldest child, Joan, was six years older than me, and middle sister, Allison, was three years older than me. (Our brother Jon came along six years after I was born.) I remember looking out the window at fields and silos, stopping at Embers in Elk River for burgers, and my father singing swing era hits like "Sentimental Journey" as he drove. Like river water, Dad traveled with a song.

My enduring interest in First Nations cultures began at the trading post of the Mille Lacs Band of Ojibwe, where our family often stopped on the way to Bay Lake. As a toddler, I observed the people who worked behind the counter or demonstrated beading or other skills, and when a gray-haired Ojibwe man smiled at me, I felt seen, as if I belonged.

As I got older, I liked looking through the store's maple candy, sweetgrass, and birch bark items for sale. In a small museum, life-size, dark-wigged mannequins demonstrated what an Ojibwe (aka Chippewa) family would be doing throughout the year, such as harvesting wild rice in autumn, snowshoeing in winter, and gathering berries in summer. Influenced by stereotypes such as the Tonto character on *The Lone Ranger* TV show, I imagined myself in a wigwam home with the mannequins coming to life.

I was so fascinated by the place that my mother asked if I'd like to decorate my room "like a Native American princess." I said yes but couldn't picture what that entailed beyond a fine collection of tiny birch bark canoes and a pelt of soft rabbit fur. I wasn't sure what I sought from the Ojibwe trading post, but I knew home decor was not it. From an early age, I looked beyond my own WASP culture for alternative perspectives. I sensed other ways of being and knowing that could, and would eventually, open my mind and world.

As Mom and I shopped, we did, however, both carry a torch for the fashion and historic designs from Pendleton Woolen Mills. I liked to have their striped blankets on my bed, and Mom favored their classic blazers for her later work as a librarian. When my mother died in 2010, I provided the undertaker with her burgundy Pendleton pantsuit for her to wear on her journey. Argentine author and librarian Jorges Luis Borges imagined "Paradise to be a kind of library," and I imagine Mom in her wool suit, keeping the celestial collections organized and free to all.

At Old Orchard, there was nobody my age. Even our dog had our cousins' dog, Andy, for company. My parents were occupied with each other and with the other adults who shared the lakeside farmhouse with us—my aunt, uncle, grandparents, and great-grandmother. Sometimes Dad would take me fishing in the early morning or my grandmother Helen Wolf would sit with me in the evening. But when my sisters paired up with my cousins, I hung around the edges of their activities or went off to play on my own.

I liked to wander past the old apple trees and into the meadow, which once provided hay for farm animals. Nowadays deer ticks carrying Lyme disease are a problem in northern Minnesota, but back then I only had to pluck off the occasional wood tick, which was no big deal. Chipmunks scurried by and loons called from the lake. I'd lay on my back and watch sunlight filter into my green sanctuary of tall grass, or I'd make homes for troll figures I'd collected from Paul Bunyan Land in Brainerd.

I tried to fit in by playing the roles available in my family, such as being a helper or clown. I was a source of amusement, like any kid could be. One day, Joan and our cousin Rick told me Casper the Friendly Ghost lived in a lumpy mattress in the attic and wanted me to bring him food. I played along, picking wild raspberries as offerings to the cartoon spirit. I even asked Mom to buy a bag of M&M's for Casper when we went to the store. When I brought the berries and candy to Joan and Rick, they informed me the ghost would not eat with me around. They then disappeared, giggling, up the creaky attic steps to "feed Casper."

When we returned to Northfield, I made an effort to renew the friendships I had there, since I'd been absent all summer. I preferred being in Northfield, at least until I was old enough to invite friends to join me at Bay Lake. I liked the idea of having a home in nature, just not the dynamics of the situation at Old Orchard, leaving me the odd girl out.

My family lived on the east side of Northfield, near Carleton College where my dad worked. After my brother was born, we moved to a house on a cul-de-sac called Bunday Court. Our big sisters got the upstairs bedrooms while Jon and I were downstairs, past the laundry room. From my current perspective as a parent, I think it's more logical to keep the youngest children upstairs and let the ten- and thirteen-year-olds have the run of the basement rooms. But our Bunday Court household ran on the principle that "squeaky wheels get the grease." I felt it was my job to tend to the others and wasn't much of a squeaker myself.

My pleasant, easygoing demeanor was rewarded, so that's what I expressed. My dad's most common request was for us to "be helpful" to others, and I tried. Joan called me Dilly, a nickname that persists among my family to this day, and I took it to refer to Dairy Queen's sweet ice cream treat on a stick rather than a sour pickle.

When my grandfather, Louis Wolf, noticed me smiling, he'd recite, "Smile awhile and while you smile, soon there will be miles and miles of smiles." I accepted that rhyme as words to live by, especially after glimpsing my wet, scrunched, unhappy face in the mirror one day and finding it unacceptable. Smiling took precedence over crying; I stifled my tears.

I made no objection to my room assignment, going along to get along. My cinder block bedroom had a window that opened to the ground level of the backyard, and I often lay awake at night, worrying something or someone would come through the window and get me. My worry was exacerbated by reading a Sherlock Holmes story about a sneaky poisonous snake. I did not mention my fears, as I did not feel they mattered to anyone but me.

I had a record album of classic fairy tales and would sit by the cold fireplace in the basement, listening to *Cinderella* repeatedly, internalizing it as catechism. In my mind, I was of the hearth as much as Cinderella, who had to sleep in the ashes. I didn't know then that I would have to make my own fairy-tale ending.

The moodiness of my adolescence compounded the challenges of self-expression. I didn't know how to make sense of my own emotions or express them to others. Sometimes I felt like I had a bottomless pit in my life and didn't know how to be full and satisfied. I kept myself on the move to outrun depression.

As far as I can tell, I wasn't born with common sense. Nor did I have much guidance to help me develop any, the lack of which led to some unhealthy coping mechanisms, such as drinking too much at parties. Twice my parents dragged me in from our doorstep in the night, ignored the vomit in my hair, and laid me unconscious on my bed. They said nothing to me the next morning, except one comment from my father after the first incident.

"Watch out for that drinking, Barb."

I nodded my aching head and poured my orange juice.

In my family of origin, with the exception of one openly emotive sister, if we had feelings, we took them to our bedroom and closed (or slammed) the door. We worked it out on our own, or we didn't. I wanted a more happy, healthy, and balanced life, so I tried to figure out for myself how to find help.

As a teenager, I read *Primal Scream* by psychologist Arthur Janov and concluded I needed his therapy to address my issues. Janov asserted, "The number one killer in the world is not cancer or heart disease, it is repression."

Janov's words grabbed my attention. I was out of touch with myself and my feelings, covering up my flaws and problems. Decades later, I understand that I am probably what psychologist Elaine Aron identifies as a "highly sensitive person" or HSP. I was affected by just about everything and already developing chronic health problems. I had frequent stomachaches and psoriasis on my scalp. When I went out in public, I made sure my curly brown hair covered the scales. I presented myself as happy, healthy, and carefree, though that was not my inner reality.

I applied to get primal therapy in Minneapolis, where I planned to go by bus or college shuttle. Without a word to anyone about my plans, I withdrew fifty dollars from my bank account for the application fee. I sent the money to the therapy center, along with a lengthy form detailing why I needed the kind of psychotherapy where people sobbed and screamed out their pent-up emotions.

Like many families in those days, we had one telephone. Ours was in the kitchen, in the middle of our Bunday Court house. I happened to answer the phone when a man called from the therapy center. He sounded calm and professional as he told me my application had been accepted. He discussed the schedule for my therapy sessions. As I grabbed paper and a pen to write down the details, my parents stood with puzzled faces nearby in the dining room, watching me. It's not like I was doing something illicit like making a drug deal, so why did I feel so "caught" and uncomfortable? No one else in my family sought therapy; maybe I had breached an invisible line.

When I hung up the phone, Mom asked, "What was that about, Barb?"

Being a bookish family, more left-brain cerebral than right-brain emotive, I told them about Arthur Janov and his theories of psychotherapy, thinking they would accept, if not understand, my need for Janov's methods. I did not consider telling them what I'd written about my feelings on the application. I might have welcomed a chance to tell them of my turmoil if they had asked about my inner life. But I didn't expect any such inquiry because we were not accustomed to speaking about our struggles. It seemed we four children were expected to do well in school, pursue our interests, and put our dishes in the dishwasher after supper, not display our emotions to others.

Mom and Dad did not see the value of Janov's work and failed to recognize my need for help. My facade of an easygoing, high-functioning teenager had fooled them too well.

Dad vetoed my plan. "You're talking about major surgery when all you need is a Band-Aid." He said he would consult a fellow professor at the college about my options for counseling services in Northfield. I don't know if he ever did; the topic never came up again. I may not have needed "major surgery," but it had taken major effort for me to reach out for help, not only to the therapy center, but to explain myself, even to that limited extent with my parents.

I had nowhere to process my thoughts and emotions, except in my journals and talking with my Northfield friend, Amy. What I really needed was to leave the dark cave of the basement and holler like my life depended on it. Four decades later, I had my opportunity.

❦

During a rainy, windy week of November 2015, I holed up in a little cabin, fit for a hobbit, complete with a round Dutch door, at a writers' retreat for women on the south end of Whidbey Island. Every writer had her own secluded cabin, with its own woodstove for warmth. My daughter, Emily, lived nearby, but I didn't visit anyone while there. In the evening, the writers walked through the woods to the main house and received a home-cooked meal. After a convivial supper, we all returned to our cabins.

Back in the woods, Screaming Woman emerged. My timber-frame sanctuary was out of earshot of the other cabins. A wind came up powerful enough to blow us to Oz or at least to blow down some Douglas firs over the power lines. We had no electricity for two days, which was okay with me. It happens in the Midwest sometimes too, so I was used to it.

However, my fury erupted when the power came back on. I tried to reset the clock radio in my cabin and could not get it to work. I made an exasperated noise from deep in my throat and then couldn't stop growling. I set the clock radio down and the growl became a full-on cry from my core. I screamed and cried, but mostly screamed, till my throat was sore and I was weak with the relief of it. Long-repressed emotions found an outlet and just kept flowing. The next day, I had another private primal scream session in my cabin, yelling and punching my pillow until I was nothing but an empty vessel slumped on the bed.

I sat up and grabbed my notebook, following where my pen and pent-up emotions led me. No one was there to hear me except me. I wrote what I observed:

When I stopped screaming, I listened. Here's what I noticed.
I heard a drum moving the blood of life.
I heard the swish of Merlin's cape as he entered a crystal cave and I followed.
I heard whales crying for me in the sea.
I heard the splash of water on my body.
I heard wind whistling and flames crackling.

My hearth is lit.
In the crystal cave, the glass slipper melted in the fire and became a lens, my third eye.
I can see you now with that Buddha eye and know we are not ashes but glowing embers for each other's hearths.
I can visit the dark cave yet live in the light.
That is my fairy-tale ending, for now: light and shadow together.

I cannot argue for or against the benefits of loud ranting, but, in my case, it helped me gain access to feelings I had stifled. It was a cleansing experience to release them. Then, with my "Buddha eye," I saw glimmers of my precious self, washed by whales and tended by fairies, shimmering back to life. I began to reclaim my voice and express myself on a regular basis, more honestly and assertively than I had been doing. I was making progress, though a two-day purge did not make up for fifty years of learned repression.

3

FINDING MY WAY

My thoughts are stars I can't fathom into constellations.
—JOHN GREEN

*A*s a child, I wondered where I fit in, usually returning to my close friend, Amy, to have the conversations I craved about our feelings and what we were each going through. I've known Amy my whole life. In 1956, our mothers were in the same bridge club and happened to be pregnant at the same time. Amy and I were born a month apart. Though we had contrasting personalities—my extroversion versus her introversion—we had much in common because of our shared history. We'd find humor in small, everyday things, like getting a noseful of water at the public pool or taking a clumsy fall from our skis in the arboretum, pitching sideways in the snow. Nobody could send me into a laughing fit better than Amy.

As we got older, we spent more evenings walking along the sidewalks of Northfield, talking and talking. When I tried to piece together my hazy memories of drunken nights, Amy was there to see me through my veil of shame. When Amy was despondent and questioned her own value, I was there to believe in her.

My parents rarely noticed my subtext, but Amy did. When one truth is told, others break free. She and I didn't solve each other's problems, but we heard each other's hearts—one of the superpowers of friendship.

In Northfield and the nearby town of Faribault, I worked as a maid in an old hotel, a janitor in a psychiatric hospital, and a laundress in a turkey slaughterhouse. I had an odd fascination for the underside of life, perhaps because I no longer trusted the pretty facades of Minnesota Nice. I knew I wasn't as happy as I pretended to be and assumed that was true of some others as well. I looked for ways to escape social pretense and experience something authentic, with no frills. No way to pretty it up. As I prepared to attend college in New York, I played out my Cinderella role of scullery maid yet again.

Amy and I both worked at New Richmond Turkey Factory, as it was euphemistically called. After two weeks, Amy had to quit due to her reaction to the cleaning chemicals, leaving me as the lone female on the night shift. I went to work early one day and took photographs of day-shift activities, recording the gritty reality of killing and preparing animals.

I was a fan of photographer Diane Arbus and thought of her stark images as I documented my work environment. One blurry picture captures a man in the blood tunnel, the first destination for the turkeys unloaded from the truck. The man wears a yellow rain jacket and rain pants and carries a yellow-handled knife for slitting throats. There are red splatters on his white hat. The birds' lives ended in that tunnel. In my two photos of the line workers, plump, motherly looking women stand side by side on the concrete floor. One has turned her head to smile at me. A conveyor belt above them carries the turkeys along, hung by their necks, to be plucked and eviscerated by the women.

The slaughterhouse used every part of the turkeys, except the gizzard stones. A barrel of stones was discarded every night. Those details fascinated me, so I wrote a poem about myself as a young woman on a kind of disassembly line. In a burst of adolescent inspiration, I called it "For Margaret Atwood," thinking of the author whose first novel was called *The Edible Woman*. What was consumable and what was left behind? I was a vegetarian at the time and yet became a member of the Amalgamated Meat Cutters Union. If I'd commuted two counties south to Austin, Minnesota, I could have helped make SPAM, the ultimate amalgamated meat.

※.

After high school and a gap year, I attended Sarah Lawrence College near New York City, where my appetite for the arts and the idiosyncratic was satisfied beyond all expectations. With a diverse array of people, I felt less of a misfit, engaging in wide-ranging conversations that kept my brain cells hopping.

One Sunday, my college friend Melinda took me to a Buddhist meeting in Manhattan. At the door of an apartment, we removed our shoes, went into the living room, and sat on a carpeted floor in front of an enshrined scroll, a mandala Melinda called Gohonzon. We were among about fifteen people, including Black, white, and Asian. The meeting began with a simple chant, followed by reciting portions of the Lotus Sutra, one of the Mahayana teachings that encouraged us to act as bodhisattvas, with wisdom and compassion. I was impressed by the calming effect of the chant, *Nam-myoho-renge-kyo*, an invocation signifying the Lotus Sutra.

In 1253, Japanese sage Nichiren had identified that phrase,

meaning "devotion to the Mystic Law of the Lotus Sutra," as the vibration or essence of the universe. It seemed strange, but I gave it a try. As I chanted, I felt a profound fulfillment, as if, for the first time, I found the nourishment I needed. My hungry feelings—for attention, for men, for ever-new experiences—gave way to feelings of peace.

I chanted every morning and evening in my dorm room. When I received my own scroll, I purchased lumber to make a small butsudan, sanding the wood till it was smooth to the touch. One of the college maintenance crew kindly helped me put it together. My restless search continued, but now I had my Buddhist practice to keep me grounded as I returned to my home base of the Gohonzon every day.

Later, I switched coasts and attended universities in Vancouver, BC, and San Diego, California. I received degrees in psychology, increasing my knowledge of human nature, though not necessarily my own. The U2 song, "I Still Haven't Found What I'm Looking For," was true for me at that time. What was the common denominator of my failed quests? If I never felt fully at home anywhere, it was because I was not fully myself. I had recurring dreams that gum was stuck in my throat, and I couldn't speak. I adapted to others, trying to be supportive and fulfill what expectations I imagined they had of me. I was not even aware I ignored myself in the process. Such misguided effort to please others was not a path to enduring happiness.

When I returned to Northfield after graduate school, I rented an apartment and worked at Carleton. In the depths of winter, friends in the Twin Cities invited me to a gathering that included visitors coming by bus from Chicago for a Buddhist exchange meeting. Though it was a snowy February, the weather and the roads were clear. I drove my Honda an hour north to a home in Minneapolis, where we began, as usual, with chanting and prayers. Then we studied and discussed Buddhism.

Donald Terao was one of the visitors from Chicago who attended that small meeting; his words were few but encouraging. Afterward, we gathered with a larger group of Buddhists at a party room in a restaurant. I approached Donald at his table after dinner. He sat quietly by himself.

"Hi! You're Donald, right?" I said, remembering his name from the study meeting. "I'm Barb Wolf. How do you like Minneapolis?"

Donald chuckled. "When I was invited to take a bus trip to Minnesota in February, my first thought was, 'Why would I do that?'" I laughed. "But now I'm glad I did," he added. "It's cold here, but the meetings have been good." Having finished his food, Donald lit up a cigarette.

My parents had a cigarette habit when I was a child, and it had made me feel sick. I was sensitive to smoke and disappointed Donald was a smoker. I'd been attracted to his dark eyes and intrigued by his thoughtful comments at the study meeting but couldn't imagine dating anyone who had that habit.

I said, "I'm glad too! I hope you have a good trip." Then I moved to a less smoky area.

In the 1980s, Donald was involved with a culture festival in Chicago, drawing participants from around the Midwest. I knew Donald wrote music for the festival because some of us in Minnesota were learning his songs. I attended a rehearsal in Chicago a month or so after the exchange meeting and stayed with my friend, Cheryl, who was friends with Donald.

Cheryl and I went out for pizza, where we met with Donald and three others. It wasn't Chicago's famous deep-dish pizza, but it was delicious. The best part of the meal was laughing and joking with everyone. I found myself leaning toward Donald to hear what he was saying. Soon we were in a conversation of two, and everyone else had slipped away.

When we realized what had happened, Donald chuckled and said, "Oh, that's Cheryl for you! I think this was her plan all along."

"That's okay with me," I said with a smile. We talked awhile longer, not missing the others. I asked Donald about the music he'd written, arranged, and recorded for past events.

"The music was collaborative. Lots of people worked on it," he said humbly. Donald paid the bill and drove me back to Cheryl's apartment. He had not once smoked in front of me.

The next time I went to Chicago, I visited Donald's apartment in Rogers Park, about a mile from Lake Michigan. We recited our prayers together at his butsudan. Then I turned to him and said, "I should tell you, I can't be around cigarette smoke. It bothers me too much." I didn't say this was a make-or-break turning point for our relationship, but he may have caught my drift. Would this become a romantic relationship or remain in the friend zone?

Donald's obsidian eyes lost their shine. He stared down at the floor for a minute. "I should probably quit, anyway," he mumbled.

We left it at that, till Donald's next visit to Minnesota, this time to see me, not to attend an event. Donald said he had quit smoking, and it was making his head foggy. In between meals, he chewed on nicotine gum. He was in full introvert mode, retreating into himself to get through his withdrawal symptoms. We took a walk along the Cannon River, and he barely said a word. I missed our humorous and philosophical discussions, but

I knew it took an enormous effort to kick his cigarette habit. I felt he was doing it for my sake, so I decided to try to savor the silence and get used to it, rather than continually chatting as we tended to do in my family. Despite his temporary grumpiness, I began to consider Donald as a potential life partner, sensing a connection with him from a past life. Perhaps in a previous incarnation I'd agreed to meet him again.

From then on, we were officially dating. When not visiting each other, we stayed in touch by phone calls and letters between his home in Chicago, where he was an accountant at an investment firm, and mine in Northfield, where I was a development researcher at Carleton. I'd been dating a Dutch man, but he had returned to Holland. As I got to know Donald, I formally ended my previous relationship and focused on my new Japanese American beau. I stashed away the high heels I'd worn on dates in the past. Donald was exactly my height.

When Donald and I participated in a Buddhist event in Washington, D.C., I had a chance to meet his family, including his twin brother. They all were warm and welcoming to me. I felt a kinship with Donald's mother from the start, though I was raised in a white, middle class Midwestern home, and Lily was raised in both Japan and the racially prejudiced Western United States. She was not the type to hold a grudge.

One day in September, Donald told me he planned to go on a pilgrimage to a temple at the foot of Mt. Fuji in Japan. We were sitting on the floor of my apartment, near my butsudan. "How wonderful!" I said.

"I want to go for both of us. I'll be thinking of you when I'm there," he said with his eyes glowing, looking into mine.

I was touched by the thought of Donald carrying me in his heart to a sacred place. He was so serious, and it was such a profound moment that I said, seemingly out of context, "Are you asking me to marry you?" To this day, I don't know why that made sense in the moment. But it did.

It made sense to Donald too. "I guess I am," he said.

When we joined my family at Thanksgiving, we announced our engagement. My parents liked Donald well enough and had no reaction to him being Buddhist or Sansei (third generation Japanese American). But, upon hearing he worked at an upper echelon investment firm, my father pulled me aside to ask, "He's not Republican, is he?"

"He's an Independent," I said, not yet realizing how many ways that would be true.

I'm a small-town girl. Donald's career in Chicago was more established than my job in Northfield. I planned to move into his apartment in Chicago when we got married, which made me uneasy. Two things became clear during my travels. First, I had discovered how much I like peace and harmony. Some people thrive on the drama of *Sturm und Drang*, but not me. Second, I realized I had a difficult time with the noise, crowds, and pollution of big cities. Visiting an urban area was one thing, but the idea of living there was intimidating. Should I make the move? How would I manage such an unfamiliar environment? When it came time to adapt to married life, would my identity, tenuous as it was, be subsumed altogether? I had questions and decided to go on a pilgrimage for answers.

❦

For thousands of years, Native Americans have gone to a *wakan* (sacred) place in southwestern Minnesota, to gather stones to carve into ceremonial objects. An Oglala Sioux elder, Wilmer

Mesteth, said of the quarry now called Pipestone National Monument, "Out of all the items that we Lakota people have, the most important item in our culture is the sacred *chanupa*, the pipe."

The pipes made from the blood-red rocks are smoked during council meetings, ceremonies, and prayers. Pipestone National Monument is a place of peace for Lakota, Ojibwe, Cheyenne, and others who have treaty rights to gather the stone.

I chose to go there on my quest to meditate and camp overnight. Surely, I would be shown the folly of leaving this lush green prairie for a big gritty city.

After selecting a quiet spot in the campground, I walked by a gully with chunks of pale quartzite scattered along its length. The chunks had been removed to gain access to the deposits of red pipestone (catlinite). It took power and persistence to break through the hard exterior and reach the treasure underneath, just as I was learning in my own journey. I passed by a stream and then wandered along a faint trail up a rocky hill. I searched for a suitable spot to sit and seek guidance. By evening, I had found it.

Some of the boulders had their own personalities, and I sat near one with a craggy face like a grandfather. A pair of cawing crows flew overhead, and a few clouds flew higher still. I wondered how many others had stopped here or at least noticed this elder sculpted by glacier, wind, and rain.

I was winging it; I wanted to draw wisdom from nature but not sure how to go about it. There were no other hikers around, so I relaxed and considered how to start the conversation. I paid my respects and introduced myself, then got to the point. "Ancient One, I am to marry a man named Donald Terao and move to the city of Chicago. I don't know if I can live in such a big city! I wonder if I can be happy there."

I sat on the ground, listening with my intuition. I had a vague notion rocks and trees could speak to me if I paid attention. Soon I heard, in a mysterious way, like a bubble floating to the surface of water, "Change is okay. Change can be good."

In a place of such long memory as this quarry, I did not expect this response, advising me to go ahead and leap forward into my new life. I looked at the Ancient One with surprise. *Well, I thought, the rock said roll with it.* I leaned back against the quartzite slab behind me, still holding the heat of the day, and imagined my future with Donald. I received one more whisper of wisdom, "Be of the Earth." Then I gave thanks to my weathered friend and departed, walking under a full moon back to my campsite.

4

CIRCLES OF LISTENING

Listening creates a holy silence. When you listen generously to people, they can hear truth in themselves, often for the first time.
—RACHEL NAOMI REMEN, MD

*C*hicago was full of happy surprises for me. Not only did Donald's accounting career continue to progress, I found jobs I liked too, such as at Kohl Children's Museum, a creative and fun place to work.

Two years after we were married, Stephanie was born and then Emily, three years later. I didn't like the impersonal atmosphere of hospitals, so our children were born at home. I loved being a mom, and there was nowhere I'd rather be than tuning into our two little girls and helping them grow and enjoy life. But it was exhausting to be on call twenty-four hours a day, seven days a week. There are no days off for those of us with young children unless we grant them to ourselves. My husband was usually at work, and we had no family in the area to step in and help.

Because I wrote a local newspaper column, I needed time to work so I could meet my deadlines. Eventually, I found a solution. When a man named Paul came to install a Japanese soaking tub in our upstairs bathroom, he happened to mention he had three young children around the ages of our children.

I asked him, "Do you know anyone around here who does childcare? I need to work at home once a week."

"Yes, my wife, Claudia," he said.

Stephanie, Emily, and I went to meet Claudia and their children at their home. With the girls' approval, I started a routine of dropping them off at Claudia's for a few hours every week, giving me time to write. (Happily, the child Emily's age became her lifelong friend.)

When our daughters went to school, so did I, attending graduate school and then teaching psychology at a university. My stone advisor in Pipestone was not wrong: Change can be good. If a rock could smile, it would chuckle as I found my nature-loving, sage-smudging compatriots in the steel canyons of the city.

As an educator, I heard about a teacher training session in Oregon, Illinois, along the Rock River, with workshops on Native American perspectives. An author I liked, Ed McGaa, also known as Eagle Man, would be there, so I signed up. Ed offered a sweat lodge on our last evening together as a rite of purification, whereby, he said, "one feels reborn, renewed, and strengthened." As a person of both Oglala Sioux and European descent, Ed felt it was important for everyone, regardless of ethnicity, to learn about the ways of Indigenous peoples. He offered the good medicine of Mother Earth for everyone.

Ed put us to work collecting willow branches and bending them to form the dome of the sweat lodge. When evening came, stones were heated in a fire. Blankets covered the dome, leaving only a small door with a flap over it. About a dozen of us crawled through the low door and around the pit in the center of the lodge, finding our places on blankets spread on the ground. The fire keeper passed hot stones on a shovel through the door, one by one, and Ed arranged them in the pit. Each glowing rock was welcomed and touched with a braid of sweetgrass, releasing a scent of sunbaked hay with a hint of vanilla.

Like a sauna, the heat was intensified with humidity when Ed ladled water over the hot stones, steaming up the small space. We were sweating through our T-shirts and shorts. But Ed's gratitude for Mother Earth and his compassionate prayers with his *chanupa* made it more than a physical experience. We had a chance to say our own prayers and release emotions, along with our perspiration.

During the last part of the ritual, Ed explained how we are reborn when we exit the lodge, and he offered to give each of us what he called "a natural name." The stones in the center had lost their glow, and it was dark inside the blanketed lodge. Yet, without seeing my face or knowing my family name of Wolf, Ed chose to call me Wolf Spirit. "Wolf is a message carrier," he said. Then he taught me the Sioux way to say it.

I had multiple names given to me over the years. At birth, I was named Barbara because my mother, Joy, had three dear friends named Barbara when she lived in St. Louis. I was dubbed Dilly by my sister, Joan, out of her own imagination. Because of a French class where I was called Babbette, my nickname in high school became Babbit, used by both classmates and teachers. But the name Wolf Spirit, given to me as an adult, was kept in my back pocket. I was the only one who knew it was there, which was fine with me. Ed gifted me with a secret title that suggested a calling, a purpose, and a connection with the wild.

In his classic book *Walden*, Henry David Thoreau wrote, "In wildness is the preservation of the world," and I believed it. I would come to reclaim my birth name later when I reclaimed my life.

I asked Ed for a lead to what he called a "rainbow tribe," a community of diverse people practicing the type of Mother Earth spirituality he wrote about in his books. He advised me to find Matt in Evanston, near Chicago. Matt was the organizer of a group called Earth Wisdom Community, which wasn't so much a place as a loose organization of folks who met in Evanston or Chicago occasionally.

Earth Wisdom folks also met on the land of Watervliet, Michigan, each season to have a sweat lodge and learn from visiting elders, and I would join them there. Gathering in the dining hall of the old campground, we'd start our weekend together with a talking stick. We passed a stick or other ceremonial object around the circle of participants, and the person holding the stick had a chance to speak from the heart. The rest of us listened. Then the stick was passed, clockwise, to the next person.

So simple and so powerful, I thought. *This is what I've been missing!* Listening to ourselves, each other, and nature was transformative, and what I'd been seeking. The listeners simply witnessed the speakers with kind attention. It was not a time to advise or rescue people who expressed pain or problems. Being heard is itself a way of healing.

Circles have their own power. The sacred hoop is a sea change from linear and hierarchical ways like talk therapy or top-down organizations; all points are equal on a circle and there is infinite room to expand the circle to include more points. Participants are simply humans together, with no one person more expert than another.

Some people don't like talking stick circles. My husband, for instance, said he doesn't like the expectation to talk on cue.

I'd been waiting for just such an opportunity my whole life. *When do I get to talk? Now I know.*

....

DISTANCE

Growth requires movement.
And often, the only way forward is through an exit.
—ALICIA KEYES

 *'m a talker. I like to have conversations to connect with
*people—and to think out loud.

My husband worked full-time in Chicago, and when he was
home, he often kept to himself. Donald figured things out in his
head. As he once told me, he didn't like to talk about his decisions because he didn't want anyone to "influence" him. This
often left me in the cold, my advice and feelings unheeded.

Though emotionally impoverished at times, our marriage
was still studded with treasures, some more hidden than others.
When I was on the brink of giving up on my spouse, he would
get creative and surprise me. For instance, when our younger
daughter, Emily, was turning seven, she and her sister, Stephanie,
thought it would be fun to have a backward party, where guests
arrive at the back door and play games like Remove the Tail
from the Donkey and knocking candy off the *outside* of a piñata.

On a Friday evening, the girls and I prepared for the next
day's party. My husband sat nearby playing guitar. "Donald," I

said, "would you hang the donkey poster on the wall?" He simply looked at me and then went to watch television.

He seemed so detached from the family, it made me sad. But the next day I was impressed by Donald's commitment to the backward theme when he showed up for the birthday party wearing underpants on the outside of his jeans.

Ten-year-old Stephanie took one look at his outfit and clapped her hands over her eyes, moaning "Oh, Dad! No!" The younger children, however, found it hilarious.

There were some things I still liked about my relationship with Donald, such as his humor, his concern for our children, and his far-sighted perspectives, but it was not a match of compatibility. I believe it was a match made by my own karma, with opportunities for me to expand and strengthen my life. I wasn't yet willing to change partners, even when I was unhappy with my husband.

With my emotional skills stuck in my own version of Midwestern Nice, I knew I needed more clarity and support to resolve my issues. I tried many things over the years to be happier in our marriage, including individual therapy and couple's therapy. We learned the Imago therapy skill of communicating with "I" messages and reflecting back what we hear from our partner. My partner did not choose to participate in those techniques at home. A Jungian analyst asked me if I was a martyr since I was staying in such a miserable situation.

My husband and I were mismatched in both temperament and behavior. I was outgoing and had grown up wishing for more playmates, whereas Donald always had his twin brother, David.

"You know," Donald said as we ate our fried rice one day, "there was a kid named Lloyd in our neighborhood when we were growing up. He liked to come by and play with David and me, but he was too hyper for us."

"Too friendly and lively?" I asked, knowing how reserved Donald and his brother could be.

"Right. So, after a while, when Lloyd came knocking, David and I just stayed quiet and didn't answer the door. Then he'd go away."

I put down my fork and thought, *Hmm, maybe he's telling me this for a reason. Is this a cautionary tale?* I gave Donald a quizzical look and said, "So I'm Lloyd?"

With a trace of a smile, Donald nodded and said, "Yeah."

No wonder I often felt like he'd shut the door on me. I wanted him to come out and play, and he wanted to be left alone with his guitar and computer. I'd noticed over the years that Donald was genuinely interested in people. Still, he liked to give them space, maybe because he appreciated others giving him space. When I spoke with strangers or acquaintances in public, he would ask me detailed questions about them later, like where they lived and whether they had kids, content for me to gather the news about neighbors and friends.

My husband's world, first formed by his Japanese American parents, who had been in internment camps during WWII, had a narrower window of acceptable behavior than did my world of white privilege and relative ease. There was pressure for him to fit in and avoid making a fuss.

Shortly after we were married in 1983, Donald informed me that snapping at him was unacceptable. I didn't think I'd snapped at him; I'd merely raised my voice, as we did in my family of origin when we felt strongly about something. After his objection, I made efforts to modulate my tone when he was around. Even my laughter was subdued, as I adjusted myself to his dry sense of humor. Chastised for exceeding hubby's boundaries in my volume or ways of expressing myself, I felt more mousy and more constricted over the years. It seemed there was a boa clenching my neck. Would it swallow me altogether once I was mouse-size?

My friend Liz Kondo coached me to be a Japanese-style wife. Her advice? "If your husband wants you to wear a red hat, wear a red hat."

Should I grow out my wavy brown hair, wear contacts instead of glasses, dress more like an executive's wife and less like a hippie? Cuddle up to him more or give him more space? I tried to figure out what my husband wanted me to cook or say or do so we could be happy again.

Following the red hat plan was my idea, not his. Though Donald's family had maintained many aspects of Asian culture, he was Americanized over the years and never asked me to be a Japanese wife. Still, I kept trying.

I visited an elder in faith, Mrs. Masuda, to consult her about my efforts. Surely, she would mold me into a successful wife. Sitting on cushions on her living room floor, we talked about my marital troubles.

"I've been trying to figure out what my husband wants so we can be happy, but it's not working."

Mrs. Masuda sipped her green tea, then looked at me, her wrinkles crinkling in concern. "You've got to be Barbara or you're going to explode," she said.

I knew she was right, though I didn't know how to "be Barbara" because I wasn't sure who that was—or who I wanted her to be.

Stephanie completed college in upstate New York and then began working in New York City. When Emily left for college in

2007, it was cold and quiet in the house. With our daughters' absence and my husband's distance, the chill had nothing to do with the thermostat.

Donald and I brought home an Australian shepherd and a white German shepherd, to keep us company. Aside from walking the dogs together around our Evanston neighborhood, our lives intersected less and less. He seemed miles away even when we were together. Could I accept I had married an introvert who wanted more alone time than time with me?

Making an attempt at radical acceptance of my partner, I said to him one day as we prepared a meal, "You don't have to change who you are." Donald continued chopping vegetables with no response. Did I feel generous with my comment to my husband? Probably. I got so little positive feedback, I had to supply it for myself. Besides, he didn't need my permission; he was already being himself. I was the one who kept shapeshifting, such as trying to be a subdued, Japanese-style wife. What would it mean to have radical acceptance for myself?

At that time in mid-August, what would have been my parents' sixty-ninth wedding anniversary, I was thinking about how close my parents were. When they were alive, we'd celebrate their love story with extended family at their Bay Lake home. Frank and Joy Wolf lived up to their names, with a frank joy visible to all. They never ran out of things to talk about with each other. At the dinner table, we four kids joined in the ongoing discussion of the news of the day. Mom and Dad were so compatible and happy together that, naturally, I expected harmony, joy, and companionship in my own marriage.

On the positive side, my husband supported our family financially and in other important ways. He also contributed to the community, such as when he and I created an ongoing Evanston television show, *Circles of Life*. (I liked circles even then.) For five years, Donald was a volunteer producer and director for a musical production called *Haven Help Us* at our daughters' Haven Middle School, applying his musical and recording skills. Donald tended to our cars, yard, and home, and kept our bicycle tires inflated. With his sharpening skills, we never had a dull knife. My spouse remembered special occasions, such as Valentine's Day, and brought me flowers. Still, I wished for a happy relationship with friendly conversation and overt, daily acts of affection.

In 1999, Donald said he was thinking about leaving his accounting job because he wanted to have more time for his creative interests. I could see it was a dilemma for him, deciding if he should leave the investment firm and devote himself to the guitar, which he had started playing as a teen. If he left the firm, we would have to live on less, which gave us pause, but we figured we could make it work. After months of weighing the pros and cons, he made up his mind. Donald retired at fifty from his career in finance to pursue his passion for music.

I knew he was a very focused guy, but I didn't know I would become a nonentity to him as his guitar skills flourished. I became second fiddle, or excluded altogether, in the process. Donald, already a quiet man, grew even more distant. Most days, he was in his soundproof studio, practicing guitar. I felt like an intruder there if I tried to speak with him, even to give him a telephone message. As an executive at his firm, he'd had clerical staff. Was I just a secretary to him?

"I'm busy," he'd say. "I'm in the middle of something."

I'd slip out the door, feeling like I'd been kicked in the gut. I had my own things to do—meeting with friends, teaching college courses, and taking care of our home—but his rejections of me, even the little ones, hurt. They came without apologies, and he rarely made up for them later. The damage was neither acknowledged nor repaired.

Sometimes we managed to have a sense of humor about our differences. When Donald purchased a book of sheet music called *Enduring Irish Session Tunes,* he pointed it out to me, knowing I'd get the joke.

"This one's for you."

Indeed! With my husband practicing hours a day on his guitar to learn Irish music, I endured more than my share of jigs and reels. Being a lover of lyrics, I perked up at Irish ballads, but my husband only played wordless tunes with quirky, enigmatic titles like, "Admiral's Whiskers" or "Boil the Breakfast Early." It wasn't my cup of tea.

Soon, Donald was out strumming his guitar more nights than he was home. With so many pubs in the Chicago area, he found places to join traditional Irish sessions (usually playing for fun, not money) six nights a week, Monday through Saturday, *and* on Sunday afternoons. Sometimes I went with Donald and sat at a table nearby, without even a glance from him, wondering why I was there. I preferred staying home and reading a book, as lonely as that sometimes felt.

When I asked my husband to join me in an activity, he might comply, but with no enthusiasm, and then rush back to his music studio as soon as he could. It seemed impossible to enjoy things together anymore. One day, during a walk in a wetland preserve, I was excited to see a sandhill crane flying over Donald's head and asked him to look up from his cell phone. He glared at me and later complained that I was trying to control him.

No, I thought, *I'm trying to enjoy life together. It was a bird*

with a six-foot wingspan an arm's length above your thick skull!
You missed it. His refusal to participate in our outdoor experience was one of many small turning points for me.

I began to understand how golf widows felt. Was I a music
widow? I was losing hope and giving up. Did he want us to stay
together? If so, I needed more from him. When I spoke those
words aloud to Donald, he turned away. As our relationship de-
teriorated, I missed being close with my husband. I could accept
my marriage was cut from different cloth than my parents', but I
couldn't accept the daily despair. It felt like a shroud, and I'd
become a ghost in my own home. I thought about a study of the
health and happiness of divorced people. Research confirms
marriage confers more emotional benefits on men than women.
Women tend to become healthier and happier after divorce
while men become less so. I wondered if I'd be healthier and
happier if I divorced my husband. My parents stayed together
for life. Could I lower my expectations of a fulfilling relationship
to simply exist with Donald as a roommate? No, I could not.
That would be half a life, at best.

I knew how important music was to Donald. After all, his
creativity was one of the things I'd found attractive about him
from the first time we met. It's fine to make music a priority, so
long as our marriage and family are of equal or greater priority. I
did not feel like a priority. Donald's world no longer had much
room for me.

By 2015, after years of my struggles for more balance in our
marriage, my husband and I had occasionally reached a truce
but never bridged the distance between us to be a happy couple
again. As we sat one autumn evening at Ten Mile House, an
Evanston cafe, I pushed the issue. We had just come from one of
our rare therapy sessions. Phil, our therapist, had advised Donald

on how to communicate more and better. I was not optimistic Phil's advice would make any difference, but I put down my spoon and tried one more time to hear him and be heard.

"It sounds like you don't want any demands on you. You take my requests for more quality time together as an imposition?"

"Yes! I don't want my freedom restricted in any way. I need my independence." Donald said this so loudly the couple at the adjacent table looked a little startled. I wanted to turn to them and ask for a reality check.

Did he really just say that?

I pushed my food aside, unable to swallow another bite. A mixture of pain and anger wracked my body, but I quietly said, "Then we better renegotiate the terms of our relationship; we cannot expect our requests or expectations to be met by each other. With no boundaries or care for each other, would it even be a relationship anymore?"

Donald said, "Music comes first," and took a bite of his burger. I knew he liked to work things out in his own head, without checking with me along the way. When he asserted artists must sacrifice for their art, I realized how far his line of thinking had gone. "I think I'll have to sacrifice our marriage for the sake of my music," he said.

Not knowing how to respond to this tragic vision of his future, I crinkled my brows and gave him a side-eyed look. "I don't think that's true." What more could be said? There was no denying our alienation now. Rather than considering me an asset to his life, my husband saw me as an obstacle to his creative goals.

Donald had squandered my goodwill. I had tuned into him and his needs, and my efforts were not reciprocated. I thought I had been supportive to him and his music, yet I heard no acknowledgment or appreciation for trying to keep our relationship alive. Being a fiercely independent Sagittarius, Donald seemed to interpret my attention to our marital dynamics as coercion, as if listening to and caring about me would undermine his freedom, identity, and musical aspirations.

I now grasped why artist Georgia O'Keeffe had left her photographer husband, Alfred Stieglitz, to live in New Mexico, a place she loved. It also rang a bell when I read Susan Buffett, wife of investment wizard Warren, had moved to San Francisco to live on her own. This phenomenon has become so prevalent as to have a name—"living apart together" (LAT). I was heartened to find examples and role models as I considered my options. Sometimes it's not about money; it's about happiness.

Though the marriage remained intact, Warren was sad when Susan left, stating, "It was definitely 95 percent my fault. I just wasn't attuned enough to her, and she'd always been perfectly attuned to me. She kept me together for a lot of years. It shouldn't have happened."

I recognized those dynamics in my own marriage. With that much asymmetry, something was bound to collapse. Could I find a way to move on in my life?

Closer to home, I thought of a neighbor who confided the news of her imminent divorce. One day at the bus stop, waiting for our children to return from school, she described the way she broke the news to her son and daughter about the upcoming split.

"I've about had it with Daddy," she told them.

Within days, her husband was gone from their home and the neighborhood. I could not imagine such a scenario with our daughters. I had no script prepared. But my neighbor's words came to mind on the days when I, too, had about had it with my spouse.

Was my husband willing to let our marriage die—and did I have any reason to resuscitate it? If problems and suffering are signals to change our karma and behavioral tendencies for the better, Donald and I had plenty of opportunities for self-improvement.

Through studying Mahayana Buddhism, I've learned that thoughts, words, and deeds create karma through cycles of cause and effect. Those effects reverberate across lifetimes. Karma is a law of the spiritual world the way gravity is a law of the physical world. Yet, thirteenth-century sage Nichiren asserted we can challenge our karma. He wrote in a letter to one of his followers, "Misfortune will change into fortune," pointing to the teachings of the Lotus Sutra as a way to break through karma and polish our lives.

One day, rather than succumb to depression, I sat in front of our antique black butsudan, the altar where my husband and I recited the Lotus Sutra every morning. Though I'd practiced Buddhism for decades, I'd never put it to the test as I did that day. Alone in the house, I faced my personal swamp of misery and sorrow.

Rather than calmly chanting my Buddhist prayers, I roared like a lion! I slammed my hands down on the low table of the butsudan and vowed to unpack my karmic baggage. To elevate my circumstances, I needed to elevate myself and clean up my own karma, not blame others. I had been rearranging pebbles. Now, with a deep and powerful resolve in the core of my life, a mountain shrugged. A river ran a new course. Fish rejoiced and swam free. With a single vow, a decision from the depths of my soul, my life was already changing.

Unless I lightened my karma, my problems would follow me wherever I went. I could switch partners, but, if I did not change,

I'd be dealing with similar issues in my next relationship. How do I eradicate something so deep and pervasive in my life? Based on decades of daily Buddhist practice, I recognized some of my self-defeating habits and ways of thinking. I dug deep into my life to access the power of prayer. With an awakened mind of gratitude and compassion, I felt I could raise my life condition day by day. When I changed my attitudes and behavior, I found I could change my relationships.

How could I improve my karma and, thus, my destiny? Through studying Nichiren Buddhism, I learned of nine levels of consciousness. Buddhism, after all, is as much psychology as it is philosophy. The first five levels of consciousness are my five senses: sight, hearing, smell, taste, and touch. The next layer is my conscious mind, where I integrate my senses and interpret the world. The seventh consciousness is a deeper level of self-awareness, the source of my intuition and powers of discernment. Karma lies at the eighth level, the soil for my karmic seeds. What seeds (thoughts, words, and deeds) have I planted? I will eventually see the consequences of them.

Some teachings stop there, but the Lotus Sutra postulated a ninth level of consciousness, a way to eradicate negative patterns in my life. Through prayer, I tap into the ultimate reality of the ninth consciousness where I can lighten or even transform negative karma, turning poison into medicine. In Sanskrit, sutra means a collection of sacred teachings. *Renge* in the mantra *Nam-myoho-renge-kyo* means lotus. Because the lotus produces flowers and seeds at the same time, it shows the simultaneity of cause and effect. The moment I decide to change, I am already changing.

The long-stemmed lotus thrives in muddy waters, only to bloom pure white or pink or purple with leaves that repel dirt.

Likewise, I am not defined by the muck I have been through, but by my emergence in the sun as a compassionate being who can bring peace to others—and share what I have learned along the way. I bust through stinky karma and grow as I struggle toward the light. The brilliance of the Lotus Sutra is that it empowers ordinary beings like me to overcome any problem posed by the other eight layers of consciousness, even karma.

I wondered if my husband and I had completed our karmic work with each other and should move on, but I didn't think so. (What karma Donald was challenging, I couldn't say, because he kept it to himself.) When a therapist friend, Susan Wisehart, guided me through a past-life regression, I had a vision of my husband as a knife-wielding thief in another place and time. I was a Greek textile merchant with fabrics piled on the back of a donkey, the equivalent of a delivery van in today's terms. The thief stole my donkey from me, and I did not put up a fight. During my therapeutic hypnosis, Susan gave me an opportunity to ask the robber why he did it. "Because you made it so easy," he said.

I wrote in my journal, *Donald has taken advantage of my good nature so often that I have little of it left—for him, anyway. He stole my innocence and cheerfulness. He took my donkey, as it were.* This was my karma to change.

It wasn't that I was a martyr; I was staying in the marriage because I sensed I had not yet removed the welcome mat from my back. Of course, people walked all over me! I'd learned early on to be a compliant people-pleaser. Now I needed to establish my authentic self and voice. I didn't want to miss this opportunity for self-reformation; I was reconfiguring my life.

Again, I thought of Georgia O'Keeffe and Susan Buffett. They did not end their marriages when they moved far away from their husbands. If Alfred insisted on staying in New York City and Warren in Omaha while their wives moved to locations they preferred, so be it. Georgia remained married to Alfred until his death, and Warren remained married to Susan until her death.

Susan and Warren's daughter, Susie Buffett, endorsed her parents' arrangement, saying, "Unconventional is not a bad thing. More people should have unconventional marriages." There's more than one way to navigate middle age—and a marriage.

....

6

MOVING ON

Whatever you can do, or dream you can, begin it.
Boldness has genius, power, and magic in it.

—JOHN ANSTER

*T*hings got worse before they got better. My trust was broken. I did not see any way for us to stay together, so I made a choice to change my life. I was moving on, though I didn't realize my exodus, my search for my true home, would mean moving halfway across the country.

Donald was born and raised in Chicago and was comfortable there. He had good reasons to stay in Illinois.

"I'm not the kind that roots someplace and then moves away," he said. Perhaps referring to my mercurial nature, he added, "I like to expand rather than transplant myself, and grow where I am, not be reborn someplace else."

I was usually the one who got the itch to move. After a couple years with Donald in an urban apartment, I suggested we buy a small house in Evanston, a city north of Chicago, which we did. After our children were born, I longed for more green space for us, so we moved to a suburb. By 1994, we realized the isolation of country clubs and gated communities was not a good fit with our values, so we moved back to a slightly bigger house in Evanston, where there was more diversity of people, cultures, and ideas. Sometimes we went up to a cabin in Wisconsin and even considered moving there after Donald's retirement.

But when our children went away to college, we decided to move to a fifty-five-and-older community near Chicago with swimming pools and other amenities. Donald and I bought a house near a trail for walking our dogs. Sadly, both dogs were affected by Lyme disease, and Dottie, our Australian shepherd, died. Cassie recovered, and we walked her on the nature trail twice a day—snow, rain, or shine.

I joined a sewing group, took bridge classes, and tried to find my niche—and my people. I may have seen the community as a progressive endeavor with shared resources and facilities, but my neighbors were more on the other end of the spectrum, ridiculing me for reading a book by Barack Obama, for instance, or telling racist jokes in front of me and my husband. My search for my true home continued.

A place I liked more each time I visited was Whidbey Island in Washington state. Our daughter, Emily, and her fiancé, Alex, first met in Rhode Island and later moved to the West Coast, eventually settling on Whidbey Island. Sometimes Donald and I traveled there together to see them and sometimes I went on my own.

Getting to know the long salamander of an island, I gazed in stunned reverence with each new view across the Salish Sea. One clear evening I sat on a bench at Ebey's Landing Reserve and saw mountains in three directions: Olympics to the west, Cascades to the east, and Mount Rainier to the southwest, all with frosty peaks outlined against blue sky like pages in a coloring book awaiting crayons. As I watched, sunset completed the scene with violet hues of alpenglow. Enchanted, I returned to my car with a glow of my own.

The people of the island surprised me time and again with their amiable and frank inquisitiveness. They were as curious about me as I was about them. Maybe because I was usually traveling solo, as opposed to being part of a couple, it came naturally to meet friendly folks and converse with them. As I got to know local people at writers' workshops and other events, I marveled at their kindness and lack of pretense. When I was with them, I felt seen and heard. And I was at peace, comfortable being myself.

The only movie theater on the south end of the island is the Clyde, a vintage, cozy place where I could go on my own and never feel alone. Before the movie started, I would be acquainted with people in my row, having shared some humor and discussion. The first film I happened to see at the Clyde was *Spotlight,* which highlighted the power of investigative journalism and included a talk after the show. With no explanation for his presence on the island, a man named Marty Baron went up front and sat on a stool to take our questions. He was the real *Boston Globe* managing editor on which the main character of the movie was based! His presence added gravitas to the messages of the movie and reminded me of the many engaging speakers I'd heard growing up in the college town of Northfield.

Writers I admired lived in the area, along with artists of all stripes. The first play I attended at Whidbey Island Center for the Arts was *The Addams Family* musical, which was as well done as any big city production. For a sparsely populated island, Whidbey had a surprising abundance of culture and conversation. On the island's stormy days, it seemed even the trees, wind, and water were talking with each other. I wanted to be part of that conversation with people and nature every day.

I found a realtor to show me places for sale, telling myself I was "just looking." There was a housing shortage in Seattle that extended to the islands of Puget Sound, so inventory was limited, and nothing appealed to me. Then, on my own, I happened upon a magazine advertisement for an environmentally friendly, planned community called the Highlands of Langley on the south end of Whidbey. After a flurry of construction, the developer died, leaving a third of the lots unclaimed.

While on the island for a writers' workshop, I decided to visit the site in Langley. On the way there, I drove by Whidbey Island Center for the Arts and noticed a cozy-looking building across the street with a sign that said Healing Circles Langley. I didn't know it then, but it would come to be a home base for me. Then, near the Highlands, I saw a street called East Talking Circle, reminding me of the talking stick circles I liked so much back in the Midwest. I was beginning to feel I'd found a place where people appreciated circles the way I did. I had long assumed I'd have to travel to Esalen in California, Omega in New York, or other far-off retreat centers to find my people. Now, with bird wings of delight in my heart, I was starting to believe some of them were here on South Whidbey.

I arrived at the Highlands and parked between an empty lot and a row of established houses, noting the location was within easy walking distance to both the sea and the shops of Langley. I walked around the Ross Chapin–designed cottages, admiring the porches meant to foster neighborhood chats. Then, out of a yellow cottage, a woman emerged and said hello to me.

"Hi!" I said as I waved to her. "I've just learned of the Highlands and came by to look around. It's beautiful here," I said, running my hand along the lavender lining the path.

The woman walked over to me. "I'm Diane, and I live here," she said, gesturing toward her yellow house.

What luck to have a chance to talk with someone who was familiar with the place! "I'm Barbara, and I'm visiting from Chicago," I said. I had been wanting to embrace my birth name, as a change from my many nicknames, and thought, *May as well start now. It's a new place and a new beginning.* "Our daughter lives on Whidbey, and I'm interested in finding a home here as well."

Diane pushed back her brown hair and smiled at me, saying she'd be happy to answer my questions. Yet again, I was amazed by the friendliness and synchronicities I'd been noticing ever since I started visiting Whidbey. The generosity continued when I said I liked the Highlands two-story Egret model because I wanted to see stars and mountains from the upstairs bedroom.

"Ah, there's only one Egret house built so far, and it's that red one," Diane said, looking across a grassy commons. "The woman there doesn't allow people in her house. But I keep a key for my neighbors, the Wolfs," she said, pointing to a blue house across the street. "They're out of town now. We can go inside if you like. It's not an Egret model, but you'll get an idea of the quality and finishes of the interior."

It was hard to take in all the serendipity of the moment. Wolfs? Come on, that's my family name. And having a chance to go inside one of the Highlands homes? "Sure, I'd like that, if they don't mind. Thank you so much."

In the cottage, I was impressed by the simple yet thoughtful layout, maple floors, and hemlock trim. I could picture myself living in such a home. I later contacted the developer's widow for information. A few months later, the building of the Highlands cottages resumed, and I looked for an opportunity to bring up the topic of Whidbey real estate with Donald.

On one of our trips to the island, I had my chance. Donald and I enjoy looking at property and imagining how we could make it work for us. On that basis, I invited him to join me to look at the Highlands. I'd been going to Whidbey Island for longer and longer visits, once staying more than a month there in a vacation rental. I had repeatedly told my husband how much I looked forward to moving to Whidbey, but I never said when. Donald had mentioned to me that he was thinking of getting his own apartment in Chicago, away from our shared house, part of his plan for total independence. We were both hinting at living apart but never specified a timetable to make that a reality.

I drove us in our rental car to the green-built development in Langley, and we visited two lots slated for the type of house I wanted. Looking at the first site, I said, "This spot on the edge of the Highlands is more private in a way, but it's next to Fairgrounds Road. It's usually quiet, except when there are events at the fairgrounds down the hill."

"Yeah," he said, "and there are some nettles and invasive species here to cut back." We walked to the other lot, which was on Bowery Loop near some homes that were already constructed and occupied.

"This one, Lot 13, I like better. It's farther from the road and quieter. You know what a light sleeper I am. And look, there's a common area next to the lot with a path that leads through the forest, down to the village of Langley." We stood on the edge of the property under towering Douglas firs, watching jays and woodpeckers fly from tree to tree.

"Yeah, I like this spot too," Donald said. "But I don't want to move yet. Maybe in a few years."

"Yeah," I said, not wanting to appear too pushy. Getting another home was a lot to ask.

"Also, I don't think Cassie would like the long trip out here," he added, referring to our shy homebody of a dog.

"Well, I'm ready to move now," I said. "I feel at home here."

After a moment, Donald spoke up. "If you want to get this lot, go ahead. It's a lot of work to build a house from scratch. You'll have to supervise, often from afar."

Make all the design choices myself? I was happy to agree. "Yes, I'll do that," I told him. I felt a sense of relief at the prospect of having separate homes and wondered if that relief was mutual. I couldn't wait to get started.

That's when pronouns became problematic. Was it "we" or "I"? Would I be living on Whidbey by myself? I pictured living in Langley alone while Donald lived in the Chicago area. We'd have our separate spaces, though we'd go back and forth for holidays and family events. Donald expected me to sell stocks I'd inherited to buy the lot and start construction, which I did. I relied on Donald, the high-wage earner in our household, to pay the rest from our joint account, which he did. So, it was *our* house, yet it felt like mostly *mine*.

I didn't know if our marriage would last. The weight of daily discord and acrimony was too much, and we could not go on as a couple the way we were. Though unspoken, Donald and I were leaving each other. Or, at least, I was leaving him. For me, it was not so much about losing my husband as it was about finding myself—and living my vow to change my self-sabotaging karma.

Even with multiple unknown factors, I trusted my reasoning and intuition informing my decision to move. I had befriended my inner Barbara.

In March, ground was broken on our property in Langley

and construction began. I monitored the work from our home in Illinois, with each design choice stirring my imagination of what my future on Whidbey Island would be. Our imminent separation was becoming a reality, though we danced around its implications in our usual manner.

Then one May morning, I asked Donald to join me in our sunroom overlooking the pond and nature trail behind our house. After his workout and shower, he came and sat in a wicker chair near me. Cassie lounged at our feet as I served Donald iced tea and pistachios, keeping my tone light. I wanted us to talk with each other about our relationship without losing our tempers. Together, Donald and I reflected on how fortunate we'd been to find each other, have two children, and raise them to be delightful, productive people. Despite the ever-widening gap between us, we still found much to appreciate about each other and our marriage.

"You know," Donald said, "at our music session the other day, one of the guys asked me what I'll do when you move away." Donald's tone was somber. "I told him, 'I don't know. Take it day by day.'" He looked at me with a hint of tears in his eyes. "I'll miss you."

I took my husband's familiar broad hand in mine. As we sat together, I took a deep breath and watched an egret in the pond taking slow, deliberate steps through the water. Then I turned and looked into his dark eyes. "You're the person closest to me in the whole world," I told him. "This is not easy for either of us. I'm changing and my life no longer revolves around our kids or even you. I need to be my own person. But I'll miss you too."

I asked Donald if we could replace my gold engagement and wedding rings and he approved. My fingers and joints were bigger than they used to be, and now the rings were too small. Also,

I rarely wore gold and wanted to get silver-toned jewelry, which suited my taste better. We went to a jeweler who moved the diamond from the prongs of my Tiffany setting to a band of white gold. No matter the setting, the central diamond remained, and I found the symbolism comforting. As for a silver wedding ring, we bought a used one with a simple, basket-weave design. I suppose it was from a divorced or deceased person, but it fit my style and my finger, so I was happy. It was refreshing to make choices based on knowing myself and what I wanted. Donald asked the jeweler to inscribe our wedding date, March 26, 1983, inside. Then, like when we were married, Donald slid the wedding ring on my finger and kissed me.

In late August, Donald and I packed a sofa, dining room set, and half my clothes into an eight-by-ten-foot trailer hitched to our Subaru Forester. We drove on Interstate 90 from Chicago to Seattle. I made a point of taking pictures of the two of us in each of the eight states we passed through, including Minnesota ("No," I said, "I don't want to stop in my hometown.") and South Dakota ("No," he said, "I don't want to stop at Mount Rushmore."). We remained civil, taking turns driving and sticking to the task at hand: get to the West Coast with no collisions of our emotions or our trailer.

When we reached the Salish Sea (aka the Puget Sound), we took a ferry to Clinton. How happy I was to see the Welcome to Whidbey Island sign as we disembarked! We drove ten minutes more and arrived at my little Lot 13 house in Langley. A few days later, we returned the trailer, I kept the car, and Donald flew home to Illinois.

He left one of his guitars and an octave mandolin in the closet. He'd be back, eventually.

7

MAKING IT HOME

Wise people fashion themselves.
Not a mother, not a father will do so much, nor any other
relative; a well-directed mind will do us greater service.
—SHAKYAMUNI BUDDHA, *DHAMMAPADA*

When our house in Langley was almost completed, I moved into it. When would my husband and I see each other again? Would we even *want* to see each other again? Would I like living on my own, or would I be spooked by every little noise and flummoxed by every mechanical problem?

Before I moved, I had weighed the risks of living in northwest Washington. I would be trading the tornadoes of Illinois for volcanoes and fault lines. Washington was overdue for a major earthquake and tsunami along the Cascadian Subduction Zone. In addition, I had an astrological map that showed planetary influences for me, a Gemini. A Sun sign ran through the Midwest at the time of my birth, indicating a fortunate place for me to be. Not so fortunate was the Neptune line running near Whidbey Island. The booklet provided by the astro-cartographers predicted dangers and difficulties beyond my control if I were to live near that line.

Neptune, a spooky, sad sack of a planet, can enhance intuition and spiritual pursuits, which is good, but comes with the danger of blurring the boundaries between fantasy and reality. "Health problems seem to occur to many in this zone. . . . You need to find a like-minded group of supportive peers to sustain your identity against a barrage of negativity." The cautionary descriptions continued, some specific and some rather obscure. "This zone exudes a vague, depressive, gray-like atmosphere." According to astrology, the island would be, at best, murky and, at worst, full of dangers.

The climate of the Pacific Northwest was, indeed, often murky and damp. But the atmosphere was the opposite of depressive for me. When I was there, I felt as close to content as I'd ever been. I explored the forests and bluffs every chance I got, even in the rain. Meanwhile, I made sure my water heater and house foundation were strapped down in case of a shake-up. I also stocked up on water, food, and other supplies. Our island is accessible by a bridge on the north end and by ferries to two points on the island, Coupeville and Clinton. All of those would be affected by a major disaster, such as an earthquake. We could be cut off from the mainland for weeks or even months.

Whidbey, previously given the Salishan name, Tscha-Kole-Chy, is a fifty-seven-mile-long, mostly rural island covering 168 square miles. Indigenous people once raised woolly white dogs on the island and wove blankets from their fur. Now, Snohomish and Lower Skagit people continue their canoeing and fishing traditions from towns and reservations nearby. The city of Oak Harbor on the north side of the island is dominated by a naval air station with Growler jets swooshing overhead. Near Oak Harbor is Deception Pass State Park and a bridge to Fidalgo Island, which, in turn, has a bridge to the mainland. Deception Pass Bridge is a popular tourist attraction and one of the most photographed sites in the state. When I first walked on the bridge, my stomach dropped as I looked down to the sea far below.

Ebey's Reserve, with its sweeping views of farms, mountains, and the Salish Sea, takes up the middle of the island. On the south end, many of the residents of Freeland, Langley, and Clinton commute by ferry to the mainland or are retired. In the summer, visitors flock to Whidbey beaches, art galleries, and restaurants.

Emily, already living in Freeland, took me to Double Bluff Beach near her home. I had expected a golden sand beach and was a little disappointed to see how gray and rocky it was. Then I went scrambling over piles of driftwood and looked more closely. As I walked on the shore, I picked up stone after stone, each more beautiful than the last, varying in color from dazzling white to red, green, gray, striped, and solid black. Translucent agates caught the light like gold nuggets.

Farther down the beach, I encountered erratic boulders taller than me, deposited by glaciers seventeen thousand years ago, the same glaciers that carved out the sound where Emily and I stood. Across the water was evidence of the volcanic nature of this landscape; snow-topped Mount Rainier was clearly visible, though one hundred miles away. We also saw the skyline of Seattle, thirty miles away as the crow flies. I could picture myself taking walks down the curvaceous, two-mile-long beach on a regular basis.

I knew I needed my own space to catch up with myself, and I needed remedial education, starting with my own emotions. In the quiet of the new house, I took time to notice my inner conditions. *Oh, I have a feeling! Let me sit with that a minute.* Getting to the level of the "terrible twos," the phase when toddlers wield the power of refusal, was progress for me. I reveled in my new-found ability to say no. I wanted to stamp my foot and say no when the builders asked if they could show my place to those interested in buying one of their similar new homes. I considered what bothered me about it, and it was the idea of my floors and rug getting dirty. So, I said yes, as long as people removed their shoes when they came in the house. I was getting better at setting reasonable boundaries.

In my Langley home, I could weep or rant as needed. I was surprised that letting myself feel sad or angry for even a brief time helped me move through my day with more clarity and peace. It was a relief to take a minute for myself, such as lowering my head and sobbing or making whatever noises helped me express myself in the moment. Like clouds on a breezy day, emotions passed quickly when I gave them a voice. After a while, I could tune into myself and tune out others' expectations and energy, as needed.

I was not the type of person who required company. I liked being with people who enjoyed being with me, but being alone was good too. I found feeling lonely while living with someone is more painful than living alone. I cherished the haven of my Whidbey Island cottage where I could tune into my inner life. I saw Mount Baker, snow-covered year-round, out my bedroom window. I needed to be in nature and could now travel to the mainland to hike among mountains or walk out my door to go to a forest or a beach. I planned to immerse myself in the rustic beauty of the Pacific Northwest.

Prior to moving to the island, I planned and designed the interior of the Egret cottage, simple as it was, selecting recycled materials for countertops and a silky slab of a local, fallen Sequoia for the snack bar. The interior colors for my island home were white walls with aqua cupboards and furnishings. I wanted a blue exterior as well, but both our daughters recommended charcoal gray instead, so we went with that. I trusted their judgment. Plus, I wanted them to like the house as much as I did.

The exterior painting was only half done when I moved in, though we'd made our final payments on the real estate transaction. In the laid-back fashion of the island, a soft-spoken bearded fellow named Larry would show up from time to time and paint for a while, leaving his scaffolding and ladders in place for his next sporadic visit.

One Friday night in September, I was alone in the house getting ready for bed. (Donald, as usual, was in Illinois.) After reading for a while, I turned off the light to go to sleep. About ten minutes later, I heard rattling and scraping noises. My eyes flew open. It sounded like feet scuffing on the steps of an aluminum ladder. Was someone climbing up to my second-floor bedroom? Without thinking, I got out of bed and went to look out the east window. In the dark, I dimly saw a figure, about an arm's length away. A man was climbing the ladder Larry had left on the side of the house!

I raised the window and channeled my father's voice at his most stern. "What the hell are you doing?"

The climbing man said, "Looking to see what's up here." He spoke as if he was having a casual conversation rather than caught in a transgression.

"Well, get out of here!" I slammed the window shut.

Then I called 911 on my cell phone. An officer from Langley arrived within minutes and searched the yard and my garage with his flashlight. Then two more police cars showed up, and I went outside in my robe and slippers to speak with the officers. Several cottages were under construction across the street, and tools had been repeatedly stolen from the site. The police officers hypothesized the ladder climber was searching for portable property to steal, not me. He probably didn't plan to enter the house or attack me. They never found the trespasser but did place the tall ladder on the ground so it couldn't be used so easily.

When the police left, I went back to bed, but was too shaken up to sleep. I felt vulnerable and wished Donald and our German shepherd, Cassie, were with me. I finally dragged my blanket into the bathroom, locked the door, and slept on the floor. I felt safer there.

In the light of morning, I was calm again, sensing I had been tested and passed. I chose this new life and wasn't about to be scared away. I was not only learning to listen to myself, I spoke up for myself! My actions to face a potential intruder were a far cry from when I lay in my childhood bed, staring at my basement bedroom window, cramped up with fear of some unknown invader.

Was the ladder incident also an opportunity to break through my karma? When I thought back to my vision of a past life when a thief stole my donkey, I recalled how I let the robber take off down the path with my animal and my textiles, the merchandise I was selling, without a fight. This time in Langley, I confronted the intruder and saved my ass, or at least the workers' tools, if there were any to be had. I discovered I'm stronger than I knew. I have a voice.

I went to the hardware store to look for motion detector lights and happened to see Larry the painter there, which was good timing. I caught his eye and said, "Hi, Larry! I'm glad I ran into you because I need to tell you something." I considered my words, staring blankly at some coils of wire on the shelf next to me.

Perhaps he could tell by my tone that something was amiss. "Oh, no, what is it?" He grabbed his chin with his right hand as if to affix his beard there, concern in his eyes.

I didn't want to sound accusatory, but I needed to tell him. "Somebody was using your ladder to climb up to the scaffold near my bedroom window last night," I said. "The police came and checked it out, but they didn't catch him."

"Oh, my gosh! I'm so sorry about that! I'll take care of it," Larry said. He turned to go, took a few steps, then looked back at me. "I'll take care of it," he said again and went out the door. Before the day was over, Larry had removed all his scaffolds and ladders, only using them in the daytime and putting them away at night. The dark gray house with white trim looked sturdy, neat, and dignified when he was done.

❦

Family is what you make it. That weekend, I hosted what I, unable to avoid alliteration, called September Second Sunday Suffering Succotash Supper. It became a monthly tradition from then on, simply called Second Sunday Supper, which sometimes was actually a brunch. From being an adaptable third child, trying to fit in with my family's expectations, I'd become more proactive in making my own choices, establishing a vital rhythm to my days.

It seems the more we get to know ourselves, the more we can speak up loud and clear.

Emily and her fiancé, Alex, came over with corn on the cob. I prepared ratatouille, chicken, and chickpeas with radicchio. It felt safe and cozy to be together with loved ones, just doing ordinary things. We talked and even joked about the attempted theft, with a little shock that something like that could happen on Whidbey Island; then we let it go.

Alex put up a rod for the living room curtains. Emily and Alex helped me bring two thrift store bookshelves into the house from the garage. As far as furnishings, my home was as spartan as a monastery, though I did purchase a TV, which sat in the living room awaiting connection by Whidbey Telecom. Emily, Alex, and I shared a cake made by one of their friendly neighbors, Sooja, and topped it with berry ice cream and local loganberry sauce. I was starting to feel at home in a sweet new way.

We continued to get together each month, with the young ones doing their laundry and lending their muscles and know-how to help me set up my home. We developed a routine of having a delicious meal and then watching a movie on TV. After working on their farm all day, Emily and Alex liked to stretch out on either end of the sofa, with their feet meeting in the middle, and doze off. In my Lot 13 Egret home, we could all relax and refuel in our own ways.

What was this new feeling of ease? Had I found my own personal island of misfit toys where I belonged at last?

If you are only amusing others or playing roles, it's a stage, not a home. If you're only serving others, it's a job, not a home. Where you can hear yourself and be heard, that's home.

8

A SECOND LOOK

*Sometimes it takes a wake-up call like cancer to bring us back
to ourselves. The crisis of illness may shake us free of the life
that we have created and allow us to begin a return to the life
that is our own.*

—RACHEL NAOMI REMEN, MD

I went back to Illinois in November for Thanksgiving.
Emily and Alex stayed home to care for their sheep and
geese. Our holiday gathering would be me and Donald with our
daughter Stephanie and son-in-law John. Meanwhile, Donald
and I were in truce mode, each of us preoccupied with forging
our individual paths while still maintaining an emotional home
base for our children. We acted out our habitual roles as we prepared for the holiday. Donald ordered a free-range Bourbon Red
turkey and researched ways to prepare it. I made up the bed in
the guest room and checked in with friends and neighbors I
hadn't seen in a while.

When people asked me about our living arrangement, I'd
say I was on Whidbey to be near our daughter, Emily, and my
husband and I went back and forth between our homes. Neither
of us said we were officially separated because we had done

nothing to make it official. In my own mind, however, I had a growing certainty I wanted to live in Washington, not Illinois.

I needed to take care of some final tasks in the Chicago area before legally changing my state residence. It had been two years since I had a mammogram, and I decided to make use of my Illinois health insurance one more time before switching to a plan in Washington. I went to my old clinic, had my breasts examined, and then checked it off my list.

At some point that week, I got a call from the clinic, telling me to go to Gavers Breast Center in Crystal Lake for more tests. I didn't think much of it because I had been called back after past mammograms for testing that never amounted to anything. My breasts aren't considered dense, but they tend to have benign cysts that require a second look. I expected the same situation with this visit.

It was Monday when I drove to Gavers Center, a step up in care from the clinic where I had my routine scan. While aligning me with the magnified mammogram machine, the technician asked me about my holiday plans. I told her, "It will only be four of us this year. Fortunately, they're all good cooks, so I only have to make the wild rice and pumpkin pie!"

The technician laughed and said, "You're lucky." But once she had the images ready for the radiologist, her mood changed. She stopped talking and wouldn't look me in the eye. My heart sank as I followed her to the ultrasound room, bracing myself for what was to come.

The ultrasound technician had me lie down, then smeared some lubricant on her wand and started running it over my chest. As I lay on the examining table, the radiologist, Dr. Miller, walked in the room. She'd seen my mammogram images and wanted to talk with me. The ultrasound technician held her wand on my right breast, just under the nipple, so the radiologist could see an area of milk ducts and tissue. Then, unlike the mammogram technician, Dr. Miller looked me right in the eyes. In fact, she leaned over me with so much concern in her brown eyes that she had my complete attention. She explained there were micro calcifications in my right breast that can be indications of cancer, which is why they called me back for more tests. Near the calcifications, Dr. Miller saw several small tumors. "You should get those tumors biopsied right away," she said.

With no pain or discernible lumps, I had no idea there were tumors in my body. My first thought was, *Oh, that's where my stored-up stress has gone.* On some level, it made sense that my stuffed feelings had taken up residence in my chest and turned to disease. It had been building up for years. I had just begun to pay attention to my emotions and find ways to express them. I suspected my healing journey would require much more than awareness, but it was a start: Get clear about who I am and what I need so I can be healthy.

Why did I get cancer? There I was, living my ordinary life while cancer was making itself at home in my body. "We get mutations all the time just by living on this earth," wrote breast cancer specialist Dr. Susan Love in *Dr. Susan Love's Breast Book.*

Scientists don't understand all the origins of cancer but have identified biology, toxins, and diet as likely factors. We humans have altered our foods, beauty products, and environment so rapidly, how can we know all the changes we've triggered in our bodies?

Yet stress was the risk factor that came to mind when I considered the context of my life leading up to the discovery of my tumors. I recognized my ordeals and ongoing distress as contributing factors, as do many people with cancer, according to

David Servan-Schreiber, author of *Anticancer: A New Way of Life*. A healthy immune system, including its natural killer (NK) cells, detects and disables cancer. Stress may not directly cause cancer, but it often weakens immune function, making us more susceptible to disease. Dr. Servan-Schreiber wrote of a study following women with ovarian cancer, "Those who felt loved and supported and who kept up their morale had more combative NK cells than those who felt alone, helpless, and emotionally distraught." This initial understanding was further impetus for me to redirect my life. Having a theory regarding the origin of a problem at least keeps us on the path of solving it.

I got dressed and was sent into a room for what I assumed was some kind of counseling. A woman in a pink blouse gave me a pamphlet about breast cancer and tried to discuss my situation with me. I may have disappointed her because I was not ready to be inaugurated into the pink ribbon parade or process my emotions with myself or anybody else. It takes time and privacy for me to access feelings.

When I escaped the pink lady, I asked the office staff if they could squeeze me in (a little mammogram humor) for a biopsy somewhere before I left town. They said with the holiday, there was no way. Since Thanksgiving was three days away and my flight back to Seattle a few days later, I realized I would have to follow up when I returned to my new home on Whidbey.

Later that day, I told my husband I had tumors in my breast that needed to be checked for cancer.

"Where will you have that done?" he asked. In his practical way, his concerns first turned to how I would find insurance coverage and the medical procedures I needed.

"I'll have to figure it all out when I get back to Washington," I said, feeling overwhelmed already.

That night, kindness came over him. As I lay in bed, unable to sleep, Donald reached out and took my hand.

"You'll be all right," he said.

My father waited until he had his actual confirmation of lung cancer in 2000 to tell my siblings and me about it. Dad sent the terrible news by email. I remember the email because the earth dropped out from under me when I read his words. He died that July. In this case, my message to my family was more of a heads-up than a dire diagnosis.

I called each of our daughters to tell them I would be tested for cancer. Emily was on Whidbey Island, and we agreed to talk more when I returned to my home there. Stephanie was in New York City, and we'd be seeing each other in a couple days for Thanksgiving. Thinking of her close friend's mother, Mary, who had died of breast cancer in 2014, I kept my tone light. Stephanie responded in kind. "I hope it's nothing, Mom."

"Me too," I said, sure we were both remembering how much we loved and missed Mary. Perhaps I'd be the next one in our circle of friends to face this disease.

Just knowing I might have breast cancer made me feel I needed a team of support. The core of my team would have to be my husband and our children. I was reluctant to tell anyone else about my situation. I tend to err on the side of oversharing, but, in this case, I was not ready to talk about my health concerns with those outside my immediate family. If the biopsies showed cancer, I would decide at that time whom to tell and when.

I surprised myself with my certainty about staying mum because my siblings would expect me to keep them informed every step of the way. In the past, I would have felt compelled to anticipate others' expectations and meet them. Instead, I made my wants and needs the highest priority. With that decision, I was taking another step to listen to myself, know my boundaries, and "be Barbara." I suppose secrets confer power on the secret keeper—the power to withhold or spill the beans. I needed that power for myself as I faced uncertainty about my future.

The next day Donald and I picked up my medical records from Gavers Breast Center, then went to a movie, *Arrival*. It was about two different species, aliens from outer space and humans, trying to communicate with each other.

"Sounds like us," I said to Donald.

"Yeah, and which one of us is from outer space?" he asked.

I laughed at his humor, knowing it would probably be me, at least in his eyes.

Stephanie and John arrived from New York. I was happy to see them, though I was in a contemplative mood. When we sat down for our Thanksgiving meal, I requested, "Let's have a moment of silence, like our Quaker ancestors." I sensed the presence of grandparents and guides around the table with us, which felt supportive to me, adding a spiritual kind of nourishment to our delicious feast. John and Donald's well-prepared turkey was the star. We ended the meal with my pumpkin pie and Stephanie's cranberry custard pie. I gave each person a gift of blown glass from Washington.

Later I meditated on my own. When I thought of the radiology report about my tumors, the word *housecleaning* floated up to my consciousness. I made inner and outer housekeeping part of my health plan. I was determined to detox, declutter, and let go of stress on a regular basis.

Fortunately, I'd be returning to an island home that was a sanctuary for me in a place where I felt grounded and at peace. Finding the resources I needed there, however, would be a whole new challenge.

9

....

FIRST OPINION

Don't expect to sail through smooth waters all your days.
—JANE AUSTEN

I rushed to get health insurance and join a health maintenance organization in Seattle, so I could have my biopsies.
When the diagnosis was invasive breast cancer, I felt more aware
of my mortality than I would have liked. I wrote in my journal,
*Well, death. That's on my mind. I'm not yet looking death in the
face, but I seem to have received its calling card.*

Then, three days later, I wrote, *Is death so bad? I feel daunted
by all that I must do to cure this disease. I almost want to give in to
the seduction of resignation. I can't see all the cards, so I don't know
what hand I've been dealt. Has death already won?*

Not only was my health in jeopardy, both our planet and
politics were in peril. If I watched the evening news, I'd lie awake
fretting over climate change and other troubling issues. I absorb
others' feelings or "vibes," as intuitive advisor, Sonia Choquette,
calls them. When I saw Sonia years ago for a consultation, she
said I was meant to do shamanic and intuitive work, and that I
had to be careful because I was "too wide open."

Sonia's advice fit with what I'd learned from the work of
psychologist Elaine Aron, who studies sensory-processing sensi-

tivity. When I read Aron's description of a highly sensitive person, I recognized myself. Some of us need to be extra careful about protecting our boundaries. Otherwise, we take on too much from other people. After the 2016 election, I had to tune out the flow of national news for the sake of my emotional and physical health.

In my home sanctuary, I could be selective. As I wrote in my journal, *I turn inward and the world goes about its business, as usual or not as usual. I turn away from politics and other horrifying news as I heed my own. My news is—I have cancer. Overcoming disease and preventing its return are my projects for 2017. Those are my New Year's resolutions.* With each new day, I was doing what I could to stay focused and take the next action required of me.

The next step was to meet my surgeon and oncologist. Donald was in Illinois. Emily was working three jobs and didn't have free time to go to Seattle with me. I could have invited one of my new friends, but I wanted to focus on one-on-one conversations with the doctors, so I went alone. I drove my Subaru onto the ferry and then onto the mainland, following GPS directions to the medical center in the middle of Seattle. I walked through a maze of underground corridors and took an elevator to the oncology department on the fourth floor.

In the waiting room, I felt like a leaf swirling in an updraft, unsure of where I'd land. I didn't realize how alone I felt until my phone buzzed. I slipped into the children's play area, unoccupied at that moment, and took the call. On the phone, I heard the calm voice of an old friend, Casey. We'd crossed paths many times and were even roommates during a trip to Japan, but she'd moved away to get married years ago; I hadn't heard from her since. Somehow, through the grapevine of our friends in common, Casey heard about my situation.

"What's going on?" Casey asked.

I told her my diagnosis of early-stage invasive ductal carcinoma that was both estrogen positive and HER2 positive. (In my case, both estrogen and HER2 promoted tumor growth. Estrogen is a hormone produced in our bodies even after menopause and HER2/neu is a good gene that's gone bad and joined the other side.)

When Casey heard I was about to see my doctors, she said, with the firmness I remembered well, "Look, I used to be an oncology nurse. The doctors and nurses work for you. Remember, Barb, *you* are in charge."

How encouraged I was to hear her confidence! The swirling, lonely feeling disappeared as Casey continued, "You make up your mind. Pray for the outcome *you* want."

By the time we hung up, I felt ready to chart the best course, making decisions alongside my doctors.

I was called into an examining room to meet with a general surgeon, Dr. Starr. She said she'd be doing my mastectomy. Because of the multiple locations of my tumors, she did not recommend a lumpectomy. The doctor was open and friendly, and I liked her immediately. But I had come with a list of questions and she had few answers to give me. Yes, I wanted to have surgery to remove the tumors. Beyond that, I wanted to understand all my treatments and their sequence and the reason for each one. Going into surgery blind was like starting a trip with no road map. When Dr. Starr left the room, I was more confused than ever.

Next, I talked with Dr. Chisolm, a medical oncologist who seemed to be overseeing my treatment. He was new to the HMO and new to his position. He answered my questions but was tentative about some of his answers, which made me nervous. The oncologist was the first of many doctors to utter the medical mantra, "That's the standard of care." The statement wasn't very informative; I wanted to know the research behind those "standards."

Dr. Chisolm laid out a plan for chemotherapy, suggesting six cycles of Taxol and carboplatin over the course of four months. By "cycles," he meant I would have intravenous infusions of those two drugs every three weeks. He explained I would need additional intravenous treatment, known as targeted therapy, due to my HER2 positive status, meaning I would continue going to Seattle every three weeks throughout 2017 for Herceptin infusions.

"A whole year?" I said with dismay, thinking, *I want to be on Whidbey Island, not driving to the city all the time.*

Though Seattle is not as populous as Chicago, it has plenty of traffic congestion. Aside from the scenic ferry ride, I didn't like the long drive to my HMO. Perhaps all the driving I did on the busy streets and expressways of Chicago had prepared me for this. What choice did I have? I agreed to it. "Okay, if that's what it takes to overcome cancer, I'll do it," I said.

Dr. Chisolm recommended I have a port installed in my chest rather than enduring needle pokes, wearing out my veins. His suggestion seemed like a good idea. *Plus, I'm using my lidocaine before every poke,* I thought, remembering how it helped numb my biopsy sites in December. The port was easier for the nurses too, rather than hunting for a blood vessel every time. Because the targeted therapy, Herceptin, could weaken my heart, I was also scheduled for periodic heart scans. At least I had a map to follow, even if it was limited to oncology's well-traveled routes.

Dr. Chisolm didn't expect me to have radiation therapy, but

he did say when I had completed my chemotherapy and targeted therapy, I would need to take a pill every day to minimize the effects of estrogen. Taking the pills for five years or more would reduce the likelihood of cancer recurring or spreading.

My problem was I lacked physical courage. Birthing my children at home, naturally and drug-free, was an exception. I did it for my peace of mind and our babies' wellbeing. I wanted to trust my doctors, but I found it hard to wrap my mind around the treatments they recommended. I had a low threshold of pain and was squeamish at even the sight of a needle. How would I tolerate IV needles or, alternatively, a port in my chest, for infusions every three weeks for a year? I dreaded the standard treatments for cancer—poison, cut, and burn—and here I was scheduled to have the first two: chemotherapy and mastectomy.

I researched and brainstormed ways to dodge my fate, questioning the model and motives of Western medicine. It's logical to consider a profit motive of doctors and drug companies when each cancer treatment can cost tens of thousands of dollars. But amidst the legitimate nutritional advice online and in books, I found alternative cancer treatment plans that made me cringe. None of them was convincing enough to make me abandon standard oncology care.

I often heard from or met with my oncology team as I began my cancer journey and needed to keep track of it all. I purchased a blue month-at-a-glance datebook to record appointments, medical personnel, and treatment plans. The calendar had room in the margins to make note of any side effects I experienced. Yet, even as I prepared for the treatments prescribed by Dr. Chisolm, I still had doubts and questions.

10

SECOND OPINION

Nothing ever goes away until
it has taught us what we need to know.
—PEMA CHODRON

The most reputable oncology facility in my area, Seattle Cancer Care Alliance (SCCA), was not available to me for treatment because my insurance would not pay for it. But a consultation there would be covered. If cancer has shown me anything, it's that I like to have as much information as my brain can hold as I consider my options. Until I have empirical data, I am anxious. It was time for a second opinion.

I prepared myself for the SCCA appointment by digging into books and online articles even more furiously than before. I came up with three pages of questions and concerns. Since I was meeting with a medical oncologist, a radiologist, and a surgeon, I color coded my questions. For Dr. Warner, the medical oncologist, the questions were in red: "Pros and cons of Taxotere? What is the role of carboplatin? Length of chemotherapy? If my cancer is confined to my breast, why do I need to have chemotherapy in addition to having those tumors removed?" I also had questions about targeted therapy and hormone therapy.

I only had a few general questions for Dr. Finley because my HMO doctors didn't include radiation in my treatment plan. I didn't expect to need her expertise.

For Dr. Dickens, the surgeon, I wanted to know my options for going under the knife. In green, I typed, "What course of action would you recommend for your own family member with my kind of breast cancer?" Having looked at the doctors' backgrounds online, I was already impressed by Dr. Dickens, who was a pioneer in sentinel node biopsies, now a common procedure for people with breast cancer.

I was exhausted by the time I got to SCCA. My relentless research of grim topics had drained me. A healer I knew held my wrist a few days before and said my energy (chi, as she called it) had bottomed out. I thought, *Well, yeah, I'm in the midst of trying to save my life. I don't know what I'm doing, and I don't know which doctors I can trust.* Everything in Washington was new to me, so I had to start from scratch.

When I arrived at SCCA, the nurse who took my blood pressure looked worried and said, "Don't stand up too fast, you might faint." Though my blood pressure tends to be on the low side, it did not usually merit worry, so I took it as a sign I was truly as run down as I felt. I stood up with caution. I next met with a volunteer, a woman with dark eyes so bottomless, they scared me. When she said she was a cancer survivor, I wondered if my eyes would look haunted like hers at the other end of my treatment gauntlet. Sometimes, even now, I look in the mirror to see if the light in my eyes still shines.

Once I was settled in an examining room, all the doctors entered at once. Hope reignited in my chest as I saw Dr. Warner, Dr. Finley, and Dr. Dickens crowding around me. I'd been feeling worried and confused, sending out a Bat-Signal of distress, and I liked to think the doctors were there to answer my call. Their laser beam focus and interest in me was in marked contrast to the indifference I sometimes sensed from my HMO caregivers who shuttled me through their packed schedules. The SCCA doctors had seen the reports of my biopsies, MRI, and other medical records, and quickly earned my trust that they knew what they were doing. Would they confirm the treatment plan recommended by my HMO team? What about surgery? Lumpectomy? Remove one breast or two? For that January afternoon, I was in their hands.

The nurse, with a touch of humor, had described the first part of the consultation as a "group grope," an apt term. I bared my chest and sat on an examining table.

Dr. Warner spoke first. She said, "Would you raise your arms for us?"

The three oncologists then prodded and stroked my breasts, neck, and armpits, particularly on the side with the cancer. I wondered what their expert hands would find. Earlier in my life, such close contact would have seemed awkward but not now. My breasts had received so much medical attention the previous two months that having thirty fingers on me at once seemed as ordinary as shaking hands.

Though the doctors knew where the tumors were located, they could not feel them. I had not been able to either. It was reassuring to know I hadn't been lax in my breast self-exams, but it was troubling to realize how hard it was to detect the presence of cancer, at least in my case.

When I met separately with Dr. Warner, she was so forthright about my situation, she had me in a state of shock by the time she was done. Maybe a little shock treatment was what I needed. A side of me still dreamed I could talk my way out of the harsh treatments Dr. Chisolm had prescribed. Instead, Dr. Warner talked *me* out of my strategies and wishful thinking.

"It's a lethal tumor if you ignore it." She told me it would be a tough year, but my cancer was treatable. Then she pinned her steely eyes on me and said, "Don't go off and take herbs or something."

I believed her. But, oh, how I understood those who chose the herbs, supplements, and potions of hope! Maybe some of them work, but I had to stick with methods based on data I could believe.

Where Dr. Chisolm had been uncertain, Dr. Warner was not. She gave it to me straight, like an arrow, recommending therapy targeted to counteract HER2 along with all three of the treatments I dreaded: cut, poison, and burn.

"I want to include radiation," she said, "to catch any mutations left over after chemotherapy. We don't want any cancer cells hanging around, causing trouble."

I didn't expect to hear that, but had no argument against radiation I could offer. All I knew was I didn't feel up to adding another regimen to my treatment plan. *I'm a lover, not a fighter. I'm not cut out for this!* As soon as Dr. Warner left the room, I burst into tears and called my husband on my cell phone, sobbing, "It's bad! It's really bad."

Donald, in his calm way, said something simple like, "Oh, that does sound bad." Just hearing his warm, familiar voice helped me catch my breath. I had to face it: I had cancer. There was no getting around it; I had to go through it.

After the phone call, I dried my eyes, and Dr. Finley entered the room. I suspected she'd been waiting till I stopped crying, which I found very sweet and considerate. She disagreed with Dr. Warner's advice.

"I would save radiation for later, in case of a recurrence," Dr. Finley said. She didn't recommend it yet because each area of the body can be safely radiated only once. She said surgery and chemotherapy were most likely all I would need. I was cheered by her advice, which was consistent with the treatment plan from my HMO doctors.

The surgeon, Dr. Dickens, was affable and reassuring in the way he talked with me. I felt he was considering my case as he would consider that of someone in his own family. I trusted his advice: a single right mastectomy with the option of reconstruction. I'd heard too many horror stories of surgeries and implants gone wrong to consider breast reconstruction. It was not worth it to me to have months of painful chest expansions and other procedures only to end up with a numb mound, tattooed with a nipple, on my torso. Some oncologists push women to have plastic surgery to make new breasts, but not Dr. Dickens.

"I want to remain flat after surgery, even though it will result in asymmetry," I said, and he supported that decision.

After consultations with my HMO doctors and the SCCA doctors, my treatment plan was set: single mastectomy of right breast, then six cycles of chemotherapy, and a year of targeted therapy, after which I would start taking an estrogen-blocker pill every day.

A few weeks later, the order of treatment was changed because Dr. Chisolm wanted me to receive six doses of a new drug called Perjeta, along with Herceptin. Perjeta is a targeted therapy that boosts the effectiveness of Herceptin. It turned out my insurance would not cover the Perjeta unless it preceded my mastectomy. For that reason, I postponed my mastectomy till June and scheduled my infusions of Taxol, carboplatin, Herceptin, and Perjeta (aka TCHP) to begin February 1.

My oncologists said my cancer was probably stage one, but it was hard to determine the exact size of the tumors deep in my breast. One disadvantage to having chemo first was that I would lose information about my tumors, such as exact size and stage. By the time the tumors could be removed and examined during surgery, they would have responded to the chemotherapy, and, with luck, they would have shrunk by then. But the benefits of having the Perjeta seemed worth it to me.

❧

When I got home from Seattle, I was too tired to make supper. On my sofa, I sipped chamomile tea and then sent an email to Donald, Stephanie, and Emily, summarizing my treatment schedule. By then, I had informed my brother and sisters of my diagnosis, so I sent them my schedule too. I dubbed them my Wolf Pack. I needed all the support I could get! (My siblings then took turns sending me flowers for every cycle of chemotherapy, showing their love with colorful bouquets.)

❧

Casey and I kept in touch by texting each other throughout my year of treatment. She often reminded me of the Japanese words, *hendoku iyaku*, transforming poison into medicine, meaning to turn the poison of chemotherapy into curative medicine, turn unlucky numbers into good fortune, and turn the situation around, no matter how bleak. Even if you don't like the cards you've been dealt, stay in the game, play hard, and beat the hell out of death.

....

11

YEW AND ME

*Healing is a small and ordinary and very burnt thing. And it's
one thing and one thing only: it's doing what you have to do.*
—CHERYL STRAYED

A s my first round of cancer treatments approached,
Donald came to stay in our Langley house at the end of
January. With an anxious dog, Cassie, at home in Illinois, Donald
learned to keep his visits to a maximum of seven days. We found
that, even with a diligent pet care service, leaving Cassie longer
than a week meant risking our dog having diarrhea and other
signs of stress.

Donald started getting to know local musicians by playing
his guitar with them at The Irishmen Pub in Everett. He also
took me to Seattle for the insertion of a port into my chest under
my left clavicle. Knowing I would have a full year of IV treatments, I chose the port in order to minimize pain and damage to
my veins. The surgery went well, though the site was sore for
days, and I had to sleep on my back, even after my skin healed
over the doorbell-sized device.

Donald departed on the last day of January. It may seem
strange to send my husband away when I was about to start
chemotherapy, but it made perfect sense to me. In our old life
together in the Chicago area, when I was ill with the flu or other

ailment, Donald rarely thought to check on me or bring me a cup of tea, even if I requested it. He didn't like being asked to do something, as if I'm telling him what to do or, as he called it, "trying to control" him. My husband was usually out with other musicians in Chicago or in his music studio, unavailable to me. I felt more pathetic and abandoned with an unresponsive person in the house than if I were managing on my own. I figured I'd recover more quickly without the added burden of trying to be heard by someone who didn't want to be nurturing—or didn't know how.

I was protective of the pocket of peace I'd established. As Donald prepared to return to Illinois, I felt a mixture of relief for myself and tenderness toward my husband, knowing we'd miss the familiarity of each other's presence while we were two thousand miles apart. In the parking lot of Ken's Korner, next to Island Drug Store, we sat quietly until the SeaTac shuttle arrived. Then Donald quickly gathered his carry-on bag, gave me a kiss, and departed. When he was back at our Illinois home, he called to report that Cassie was glad to see him and was sticking close by his side.

I arranged with my attentive friend, Carla, to be with me for my February treatments. She and I took a predawn ferry and had a chance to catch up with each other during the drive through Seattle. She grew up near my HMO's medical center and knew all the back roads. In the hospital room, she kept me company, quietly conversing at times and letting me rest at times.

Carla liked to tell me, "You're so brave, Barbara."

I would come to hear that phrase from many people over the course of my treatment, and it was never a comfort to me because I knew I was not brave. I was doing what I had to do to stay alive. Inside, I was kicking and screaming about this turn of events—and what I was required to do to my body. I wondered if people lauded my bravery as a way of distancing themselves from cancer and the fears conjured up by that word, and, if so, I really didn't blame them.

The port worked well as a direct entry point to my circulatory system, with only a slight pinprick sensation at 7:30 a.m. when a nurse collected my blood. The morning count of my WBC was a healthy 11, meaning 11,000 white blood cells per microliter of blood. Taxotere and carboplatin kill patients' white blood cells, a critical part of the immune system, so the challenge would be for my bone marrow to generate new ones in time for my next treatment.

At 9:00 a.m., my Taxotere infusion began, to be followed by carboplatin, Herceptin, and Perjeta. My nurse for the day stopped by the room regularly to check on me. There's a chance of adverse reactions to the powerful chemo drugs, and with Herceptin, there's a chance of heart damage. In fact, when the nurse began running Herceptin into my body, I felt a cold flutter inside my chest.

"Oh, that feels weird," I said. The strange sensation went away, so we continued with the infusion. I lay in a narrow hospital bed with the IV bag hanging on a pole next to me. With all the fluids going through me, I made occasional trips to the nearby bathroom, rolling my IV pole along with me.

After seven hours of infusions, Carla took me home. I had a quiet supper in my house, relieved to have successfully completed my initiation into cancer world. I called my neighbor, Trudy, and we made plans for the next day to visit Deception Pass State Park at the north end of Whidbey. My oncology team told me I would have a few days before side effects kicked in, and I wanted to enjoy those days while I could, preferably out in fresh air.

I sat by my butsudan and meditated on the theme of gratitude, thinking of Carla, the oncology nurses, and all those who helped me through my first day of treatments. My most tearful gratitude, for some reason, was for the workers on the Washington State Ferry that took me between Clinton and Mukilteo, one of the busiest routes in Puget Sound. Using a medical pass issued by my doctor, I had been able to go ahead of the line of cars waiting to board the ferry, saving me time and stress.

Sometimes, especially in summer, cars were in line for hours. On previous trips, I'd witnessed drivers' hostile reactions when unknowing tourists butted in line with their cars, so I made sure to hold up my medical pass in the window as we went around the waiting vehicles.

Carla and I had been given priority boarding, no questions asked. A man in a yellow safety vest gestured us to the front of the line. We parked in the first spot on the main deck, just behind the motorcycles, with a brightening view of sea and sky. I felt humbled, like a bird with an injured wing returned to her nest. Such kindness makes a big difference when you're going through tough times.

The next day, Trudy and I drove to the state park and began our hike on the north shore of Whidbey Island, zipping our jackets up to our chins to keep out the wind. As we walked on the beach, we saw the green girders of Deception Pass Bridge soaring eighteen stories above us. Cars and trucks looked tiny as they flowed across the stately bridge. Trudy, a creative soul, savored the sights and sounds, finding purple mussel shells and rocks of many hues tumbling in the surf. Feeling the gravelly sand give way under my shoes as I strode along, I felt confident and mostly healthy, though I knew that could change at any moment.

When I returned home, Donald called from Illinois to check

on me. I said I was hanging in there so far. I suggested he also give our daughter Stephanie a call because she was leaving for Hawaii the next day to work on an art installation there. Younger daughter Emily came by and brought me a thermometer I'd asked her to buy for me. We were all in touch by text or phone on a regular basis. Though I wasn't yet sharing my medical status on social media, I kept about a dozen people in the loop by sending email updates about my treatment.

My Minnesota friend, Amy, texted me with a message of encouragement: "How grateful I am that you are alive and fighting. I cannot imagine life without my friend. Take a good, happy, deep breath. You're going to beat this thing!" She knew how to make me smile. Heeding Amy's advice, I took a walk under towering conifers, inhaling their good green scent.

I relied on the love and care coming my way as part of my survival plan. When people offered to pray for me, I said yes, please do! It made sense to accept all the positive energy that was offered and to send prayers of support to those I knew who were struggling, including fellow cancer patients.

On the fourth day, my mouth and lips were sore and red, like they were sunburnt. It was too painful to drink my usual sparkly water. Even a fruit smoothie stung my tongue. My oncology team had suggested a remedy called "magic mouthwash," so I picked up a bottle at the drugstore. When I gargled the garish pink liquid, all it did was numb my mouth for a few minutes. I was more interested in something genuinely healing.

It was a major undertaking to make a sandwich to go with the soup my friend Raya made for me. Staring at my refrigerator door, I read the magnetic sign stuck there, supplied by my HMO: *Talk with your doctor about any side effects or symptoms that come up. Side effect management is an important part of com-*

prehensive cancer care. Common side effects include fatigue, nausea, hair loss, diarrhea or constipation, mouth sores, pain, rash and other skin changes, neuropathy (nerve damage). I would experience every one of those during the coming months, but it was my lack of energy that worried me after that first chemotherapy treatment.

I dialed the helpline at my HMO to try to find out if my fatigue was normal. A nurse there suggested that, if my condition persisted, I go to a doctor or the emergency room to be examined. This was one of many bits of generic advice offered to me when I called the twenty-four-hour consulting line throughout my treatment, most of it ineffective at helping me find relief.

Emily, who lived nearby, came over after work to assist me. We had a light supper and then she sat by my bed while I rested. When she left, she asked me to call her if my side effects got any worse.

"I'll do that," I promised, still expecting to manage my symptoms on my own.

I was not a napper. I rarely slept during the day. So, when I could hardly rise from my bed the next morning, my worrywart tendency kicked in and I assumed I was dying. This corpse-like spell made me feel glued to my sheets. I had no appetite to motivate movement, but finally shuffled downstairs and collapsed on the sofa. I was prepared to be weak after chemotherapy, but not so unwell that I didn't recognize myself.

Feeling moribund, I called my daughter. "Hi, Em. I might need your help," I said.

"What's going on, Mom? How are you doing today?"

"Not so good, hon," I said, my voice catching in my throat. "I . . . I don't have the stamina for this. I'm so tired, I don't know what to do."

"Oh, no," Emily said with concern.

"You know how I said that Herceptin could damage my heart? I feel so weak, I'm worried my heart is giving out."

"You think it's the Herceptin affecting you?"

"I don't know. Maybe I'm having a reaction to it. Do you think I should go to the emergency room in Coupeville?"

Emily came right away to get me.

At the Whidbey hospital, I put on a gown and had my blood drawn. My white blood cell count was three, a low number to be expected after chemotherapy. My daughter sat by my hospital bed, her dark, curly hair pulled back in a ponytail and her watchful eyes on me. Emily's down-to-earth presence was reassuring. I remembered her focused approach to equestrian competition during college. She memorized the course, noting the height of each jump, and then calmly rode her horse through it. Now she was accompanying me through a challenging course of my own.

I had a chest X-ray. Then a nurse pulled aside my gown and pressed sticky pads to my torso and ankles for an electrocardiogram. When she said, "Everything looks normal," I was relieved that my heart was doing fine. Then what was sapping my energy so profoundly?

I began to understand my symptoms were not heart failure but simply the way chemotherapy affected me. The powerful, cancer-killing medications sucked the life right out of me. Ten years ago, I had seen a newspaper photo of a Russian man in London poisoned by polonium-210 for political reasons. Remembering the image of Alexander Litvinenko's head inert on the hospital pillow, no glint of vitality in his eyes, I recognized my condition. Taxotere and carboplatin are poisons. My body was coping the best it could.

Emily took me home from the hospital and helped me prepare brown rice and vegetables before returning to her farm. I was worn down to a shred of my former self. I had cherished the solitude of my house so much for processing my emotions that I expected to need that solitude again during treatments. But dealing with my physical side effects was proving to be overwhelming.

I called my husband in Illinois. On the verge of tears, I told him what a rough time I was having. "I thought I could handle this on my own, but it is *way* harder than I expected."

Donald was quiet for a minute, which I knew, after decades of living with him, was normal. Still, I had a sinking feeling he wasn't understanding—or even caring about—my situation. Then, in his methodical way, he showed me he was listening. "Sounds like you have the worst side effects four or five days after treatment. When is your next chemo treatment?"

"February 22," I said.

"I'll make a reservation for a February 26 flight from Chicago to Seattle. I'll take the shuttle to Whidbey Island, and Emily can pick me up at the shuttle stop. So, I'll be there when you start to feel sick again."

"I'd appreciate it," I said. I knew Donald's friend, Nick, was in contact with him back in Illinois. When Nick found out I had breast cancer, he said his wife had gone through it, too, and advised Donald to stick by me, especially during chemotherapy. My husband, likely spurred by the goodness of his heart and whatever devotion he still felt toward me, seemed to be heeding that advice.

I had mixed feelings about relying on Donald or being helpless around him, given our precarious relationship. Could I be myself, my real self, which was my new normal since I moved to Whidbey, when he was around? He had rarely showed empathy for me in the past, so I had low expectations for what he could do for me as my side effects hit. Yet, all that paled in light of our long-term relationship—and the intensity of my suffering. Donald may not have been able to intuit my every need, but he was still my guy, my partner in life, and I needed him nearby on those days I was dealing with the worst side effects. I had Emily, Alex, and helpful neighbors around, but having someone as close as a spouse to stay with me when I could barely function would be the most comforting arrangement.

From then on, my husband made a point of being with me whenever I needed him during my debilitating cancer journey. As Donald and I were changing, our marriage was changing too. Crises reveal the character of people as well as relationships. Dealing with something as difficult as cancer, partnerships can easily unravel. Or, if we can manage it, we weave new connections as we call on inner and outer resources previously unknown.

In the evening I sat on the sofa with a cup of herbal tea nearby, trying to regain some perspective and control of my situation. I wrote in my journal, *When I get the stuffing knocked out of me, as with chemotherapy, do I get to choose what I put back in? What I take back and claim?*

I've always liked being around trees, and I remembered reading in *Science News* that the cancer treatment, docetaxel, is made from yew trees. I also remembered I'd passed the article to our babysitter at that time to give to her mom who was newly diagnosed with breast cancer. Her mother was touched by my gesture of support, which I'd come to now experience myself as a cancer patient, as people went out of their way to be kind. As I'd felt with the ferry crew and when my neighbors brought me supper, small mercies formed a cloud of love that carried me through each day.

Docetaxel is the generic name of my chemo drug, Taxotere, and is derived from poisonous leaves of European yew trees. (Taxol, a similar drug, comes from Pacific yews, found in my state of Washington.) A reliable and accurate assassin of cancer cells, Taxotere is much in demand. As part of a multibillion-dollar business, yew trees are now overharvested, as they were in ancient times when their wood was prized for archers' bows. When I traveled to Wales to explore my Welsh heritage, the only big yews I saw were in cemeteries of churchyards. I learned the toxic trees were left there to discourage cows from grazing among the graves.

I decided to think of the yew trees and their poison as my helpers and friends, and to be grateful each time I had a cycle of chemotherapy. I also decided to ask my bone marrow to make plenty of new white blood cells.

Could my WBC bounce back from its low level? My oncologist, Dr. Chisolm, didn't think so and recommended home injections of a prescription to stimulate my bone marrow following each round of chemotherapy. I considered having Emily come over and give me the shots, as she does for her farm animals. But I decided to trust my own body rather than this new drug I saw hyped on TV commercials. One person I knew was taking the bone marrow stimulant along with her cancer treatments, and she still ended up in the hospital with neutropenia, a condition of dangerously low WBC levels. I turned down my doctor's prescription, telling him I'd like to try chemo without it and see what happens. We'd know the results, either way, at the next prechemo blood draw.

As for other preparations, I purchased special socks and mittens that could be frozen and then worn during treatment. My goal was to minimize the flow of chemo drugs to my extremities. The colder an area is, the less flow of drugs via my circulatory system, and the less chance for neuropathy and degradation of my nails. In Europe, patients also used cold caps to minimize hair loss, but my HMO did not yet have the technology. Already, my brown hair was loosening its hold on my head and clogging my hairbrush. (On the positive side, my psoriasis was disappearing.) After I undressed for my shower, I took a photo of myself in the bathroom mirror so I could remember what my hair and body used to look like.

When I returned to my HMO for my second round of chemotherapy, the morning blood draw showed my white blood cell count. Dr. Chisolm looked at me a little wide-eyed and said, "It's abnormal." I expected him to say the levels were too low to allow me to proceed with chemotherapy that day, but instead he said, "Your white blood cell level is 14.7, which is abnormally high!" He was surprised.

With a smile, I patted my forearm in gratitude for my bone marrow. "I told my blood cells to bounce back," I said. "I guess they did."

Recovering from a heart attack, author and medical researcher Norman Cousins wrote, "I thought that I had a great heart and that it was doing everything—and more—that anyone could ask of it. Life has many prizes, not the least of which is having confidence in one's physiological endowments and their responsiveness to one's deepest needs." It was good to know that, even after the setback of a cancer diagnosis, I could find ways to trust my body again.

12

CIRCLES OF HEALING

Though the word may suggest otherwise,
recovery is not about salvaging the old at all.
It's about accepting that you must forsake a familiar self
forever, in favor of one that is being newly born.
—SULEIKA JAOUAD

My old self, the one who sought primal therapy and was shot down, had little confidence in my network to catch me when I fell. For instance, when Carla was hugely supportive to me as I faced cancer, I considered it a fluke, an anomaly, because I assumed my karma was to be left to cry it out in my crib as a baby and then flounder on my own as an adult. I had played out that pattern in my marriage, feeling ignored and depending on myself for the most part. Despite evidence to the contrary, with medical staff, family members, and friends meeting my needs, I maintained this assumption that "nobody has my back" even after I moved to Whidbey Island. This was neither true nor rational, yet was deeply ingrained in me.

One of the wonders of Whidbey was that when I needed things or people, they would often appear at just the right time, as surely as, in my childhood, loons on the lake answered my ululations to them from the shore. For instance, at the end of November 2015, on my last day visiting Emily and Alex before returning to Chicago, I was frustrated by my fruitless search for a home on the island, so I prayed to find the right place. Tidying my hotel room, I was about to discard a local publication when I noticed an advertisement for the Highlands of Langley. Discovering the ad led me to the site for my dream cottage.

Or the time in 2017 when Linda, a neighbor I hardly knew, appeared at my door with a beautiful Romanesco-topped dinner in a bowl when I was going through treatments and not feeling up to cooking. It turned out that she'd gone through cancer too. Or how the eagles soaring above the beach came closer when I sang to them. Or how often a needed piece of furniture, such as a white rocker to match my Adirondack chair, showed up at the end of someone's driveway with a sign saying "For Sale" or even "Free." How many minor miracles would it take to convince me to call once again across the water and expect my fellow loons to answer? At least I was starting to pay more attention to such synchronicities.

Finding Healing Circles Langley (HCL) within walking distance of my home was yet another reason to be glad I'd moved to Whidbey Island. I couldn't have custom ordered a better place to challenge my self-imposed loneliness even if I had combined the talking stick circles of Earth Wisdom Community with my favorite elders and healers. Perhaps there was something that led me here before I knew I had cancer, something in me that knew I would need such a sanctuary. It was a fortunate coincidence that strengthened my faith in intuition and reminded me to pay attention to its whispers.

I started going to HCL even before I moved to the island— and before I was diagnosed. When I was on Whidbey Island to see our daughter, check on the construction of our new house, or attend a writing workshop, I'd look online for events in Langley and make note of HCL gatherings that interested me, such as a women's circle and a meditation circle. There was even a Write to Heal circle I enjoyed, which included time for freewriting. I attended the gatherings as a refreshing change from the free-for-all interactions of my childhood where the squeakiest wheels got the grease. As a newcomer, I found Healing Circles to be a comfortable, welcoming place where I could connect with others in a gentle, fulfilling way. Everyone had a chance to be heard.

The more I accepted myself, the less I projected my problems on others. As bell hooks wrote, "When we can be alone, we can be with others without using them as a means of escape."

And as Martha Beck wrote in her book, *The Way of Integrity: Finding the Path to Your True Self,* "If you don't walk your true path, you won't find your true people." Now that I was getting to know myself and speak my truth, I sought others who were doing the same. An authentic self seeks an authentic home base, a place to belong. I felt at home with the people I met at Healing Circles Langley because of their sincerity and consistent concern for others. The goals and practices of HCL made sense to me, providing just enough structure to witness each other in a supportive way, based on the HCL "Agreements and Practices" read at the beginning of each circle:

1. We treat each other with kindness and respect.

2. We listen with compassion and curiosity.

3. We honor each other's unique ways to healing and don't presume to advise, fix, or save one another.

4. We each hold all stories shared in the Circle confidential.

5. We trust each of us has guidance we need within us, and we rely on the power of silence to access it.

Healing Circles, as a physical presence, is a wood-shingled, two-story cottage perched on a bluff in the seaside village of Langley. It once housed the consulting business of Kelly and Diana Lindsay, a husband-and-wife team who shifted gears in 2006 when Diana was diagnosed with terminal lung cancer. Their mission evolved, over the course of her treatment, from supporting global marketing to supporting the health of body, mind, and community. By the time Diana, amazingly, overcame stage four cancer, their cottage by the sea had become a haven of healing, with the couple and a growing number of volunteers providing multiple resources to individuals in need.

In addition to circles for groups, HCL also offered Circles of Two, an opportunity to speak one-on-one with someone trained to listen and be supportive. The day after my breast tumors were biopsied, I felt the need to talk about what I was going through as I faced the strong possibility of cancer. I went to HCL during the morning drop-in time, hoping to find a volunteer to meet with me. As it turned out, Diana was there and invited me to join her in a Circle of Two in the living room.

I said, "Yes, I'd like that," at the same moment a familiar, reptilian demon hissed, "You're not worthy of her time. She's a busy person! Your problems aren't that important."

I had heard that self-sabotaging message before—and sometimes believed it. This time I had a retort: *Facing cancer is an important problem, and I need help.* On the scale of human afflictions, cancer was on the serious side and even my inner doubter couldn't argue with that. Accepting my meeting with Diana as more Whidbey magic, I felt a warm, grateful glow around my heart and cast my demeaning demon into the Salish Sea below.

Because the model of Healing Circles is an egalitarian one, we met as equals, not as therapist and client. The focus of our circle was on activating my own resources to cope with my new challenges. Diana conveyed the heart and soul of Healing Circles through her humor, warmth, and calm attention to what I was saying—and even to what I was not saying. I relaxed into the sofa cushions, convinced that her sharp mind didn't miss a thing.

I spoke of my mammograms back in Illinois and the biopsies I'd had the day before. "I don't yet have the results of the biopsies, but I want to prepare myself, in case it is cancer," I had said.

We sipped our cups of tea and spoke easily with each other, with Diana sharing some of the things she'd learned during her multiple cancers and treatments. She also recommended the Yi Ren Qigong class she was teaching later in the day. It was part of the Chinese medicine she combined with Western medicine more than ten years ago to challenge her 1 percent odds of survival.

After I told Diana the facts I had so far, she handed me pen and paper to write my own health plan.

"What do you need going forward?" she asked.

I listed what I needed to release and change and what I wanted to have more of in my life. Did I write about eating more broccoli and other practical ways to fight cancer? Not really. Those were relevant, too, but did not address what I considered the root of my problem. Most of my plan had to do with being authentic and happy, such as, *Turn self-judgment and self-doubt into confidence, self-worth, and love. Let go of the need to meet others' expectations and please them or rescue them. Detox stress on a regular*

basis. Connect with family and other loved ones. Take time in na-
ture just to be. With Diana's help, I was setting goals based on
what was of deepest importance to me. In the afternoon, I made
a point of attending her Qigong class, learning how to send fresh
energy to my kidneys and spleen so as not to be overwhelmed by
fears and worries.

When my biopsy results came back positive two days later, I
started attending the Living with Cancer Circle held twice a
month at HCL, taking part when I felt up to it. After I started
chemotherapy, I was still usually well enough to leave the house,
except for the week of severe side effects.

Being part of cancer groups can be difficult. For one thing,
people in our circle sometimes died, including one by her own
choice, based on our state's death-with-dignity option. We lost
people we'd come to know, fellow travelers with whom we'd
shared our deepest fears, hopes, and pain. One young woman, a
firefighter, showed up with her husband, both trying to cope
with her sudden diagnosis of lung cancer. After seeing them
twice in our cancer circle, the husband showed up alone, with his
favorite photos of her, to tell us she had died.

"You were there in her time of need," he said. "You gave us a
place where we could be honest about this horrible disease."

When I got choked up over the phone about yet another
death of someone who'd become dear to me, Stephanie said,
"Mom, this seems too upsetting for you. Maybe you should stop
going to those cancer circles."

"Oh, my gosh, no! That's the only place I can go where people understand what I'm going through," I said. "The emotions
aren't bad, they're just real."

By the same token, I found my taste in books becoming
morbidly focused; I only wanted to read medical information or

memoirs about cancer or death, like *The Bright Hour* by Nina Riggs. When death is hovering nearby, reading about maladies and mortality can be strangely invigorating, reminding us to live while we're alive. And to love others while they're still with us.

After the knockout punch of my first chemo, I needed the presence of those living with cancer to help me process what had happened. As I walked the forest path to Healing Circles, I sang favorite songs, such as "Starting All Over Again" by Hawaiian musician Iz. As his lyrics suggest, it's not easy, but we can do it.

When I arrived at our cancer circle two weeks after my first chemotherapy, I joined six others, including Diana. During our first go-round, passing a rock as our talking piece, we each introduced ourselves and why we were there.

One tall man with a cane said, "My name is Brad. For those of you who don't know, a brad is a headless nail."

There were some sympathetic smiles in response to his poignant humor. Brad may not have been headless, but we could clearly see a deep indentation at the back of his skull where he'd had surgery.

"I'm missing a third of my brain and the tumors keep coming," Brad said. I was amazed he functioned as well as he did, focusing on each speaker with as much attention as he could muster.

During the next round, I had a chance to talk about how sick I was after chemotherapy. No matter how many times I sat in circle, it always felt like a rare opportunity to share my evolving self. When the already warm "talking stone" was passed to me, I cradled it in my palm. Then I took a few deep breaths, sensing both the patience and attentiveness of the people around me. From past talking stick experiences, I knew my words would flow more from my heart than my head.

I told them I had fatigue and digestive issues and was starting to lose my hair. "I had a *Psycho* moment in the shower," I said. "Clumps of hair came out in my hands, and I screamed. It freaked me out. I pounded on the shower wall and cried for a while."

For comic relief, for my own sake as much as my listeners, I put a hand on my turbaned head and continued, "My neighbor saw me out in the yard bare-headed and said I have old man hair. That's about right. I don't think I'll shave off my last wisps because they make me laugh when I catch sight of myself in the mirror!"

There were a few chuckles and nods of recognition. As a member of the tribe-of-the-sometimes-bald, I was not alone. I could be honest about my struggles with no expectation for others to verbally respond or try to solve my problems for me. It was enough to simply be witnessed on my journey. *Yes, this is hard. This is what is required.*

At the conclusion of our time together, Diana announced there would be a Circle of Song that evening in the upstairs living room for anyone who wanted to attend. She had integrated music into her own healing regimen and wanted to make it available to others as well. Before I got up from my chair, Brad got my attention. He fished in his shirt pocket and pulled out a business card.

Leaning toward me, he squinted through his thick glasses and said, "My wife, Eileen, will be cutting her hair soon." He looked at me meaningfully.

"Oh?" I said, not sure where this was going.

"You can have the hair to make yourself a wig," he said. "Call Eileen at the number on the card, and she'll save her hair for you." He handed me the card and smiled.

Did Brad expect me to make my own wig from the donated

locks? For one thing, his wife, whom I met in a women's circle, was a blonde and I'm a brunette. Impractical as his proposal seemed, I was stunned by his thoughtfulness. "Thank you, Brad! That is very sweet." What could I say? This man offered me the hair off his wife's head! Relying on his cane, Brad got to his feet and headed out the door where a volunteer driver was waiting for him.

I walked home, feeling lighter than when I arrived, and thought about something flamboyant singer Bette Midler said during a television interview about the perks of aging. She commented, flinging out an arm, that if she extended her hand as she got up from a chair or exited a vehicle, someone would be there to take it and assist her. Though not a celebrity like Bette, I wanted to have confidence that when I reached out, help would be there.

After a supper of kale and wild rice salad from friends Jen and Kevin, I went back to HCL for the musical evening Diana had mentioned. The chairs and sofa in the upstairs living room were pushed aside so we could stand in a circle. We were led by a rather angelic choir of Laurie, a former nun; Barbara, a music therapist; and other gifted folks who kept us singing and dancing. I was surprised how many of the songs I knew, including peace songs, Quaker songs, and even a Native American song or two.

From what I had said in our cancer circle that afternoon, Diana knew I'd be enduring another chemotherapy treatment in a week, and I could feel her support every time I looked her way. After we had warmed up our voices with old favorites, Diana approached and put her arm around me, saying she'd like to offer me an extra dose of the singers' good energy. "Barbara, would you let us sing for you?"

I put both hands on the center of my chest and nodded, wondering if I could get through this unexpected blessing without dissolving into tears. A circle formed around me, and everyone began to sing a song that was like an embrace. The exact title escapes me. It could have been the worship song "Sanctuary," adapted by Kelly and Diana as a personal pledge to be "kind and gentle" sanctuaries of support and protection for each other. Or perhaps the lyrics were by music therapist Barbara about finding shelter from the storm. Whatever the choice, it was an infusion of comfort, an offering with no strings attached. The caring came from all around and was undeniable. I was so in awe of the experience, I didn't cry.

Who knew that a loving tune could be an intervention? The singers cleared my mind of existential loneliness the way Hiawatha cleared snakes from the head of Tadodaho, a tyrant who, once detangled, became a magnanimous leader. (After Tadodaho came around, Hiawatha and Peace Maker were able to establish the Iroquois League of the Great Peace, which lasted for hundreds of years.)

People, including friends and family, did have my back. In fact, at Healing Circles that night, I had *all* sides of me covered. The emotional nourishment would carry me forward for a long time.

Fred Rogers, of *Mr. Rogers' Neighborhood*, assured us, "Anything that's human is mentionable, and anything that is mentionable can be more manageable. When we can talk about our feelings, they become less overwhelming, less upsetting, and less scary. The people we trust with that important talk can help us know that we are not alone."

I noticed that being real with others hastens healing. On Whidbey Island, I found people who accepted me—and even loved me—as I was. When you find yourself surrounded by pure-hearted love, take it in. Believe it.

13

MARITAL ARTS

*Her frustration is inevitable, no matter how much she
loves me. But that's how it goes, especially in neurologically
mixed marriages such as mine.*
—DAVID FINCH

The outpouring of support at the Circle of Song held me
in a soulful embrace long after it was over. When I was
afraid or distressed, my healing community sustained me. However, while I may have been thriving in the glow of generalized
agape, love in the singular sense was often painful and problematic. The readiness of my new friends to open their hearts was in
stark contrast with my stalled relationship with Donald, which
had been feeling more like hell than heaven.

Yet, Donald was still the steady hub, the stable center, of the
wheel of our marriage. I was the tire, spinning round and round,
making new contacts everywhere we rolled. That's how I came
up with my husband's nickname. He didn't like his moniker
shortened to "Don," so I occasionally called him Hub, short for
hubby.

Donald and I had once been in love and enjoyed each other's
company, especially during our long-distance courtship by

phone, letter, and sporadic visits. As hurt as I had been over the last few years, I was not entirely pessimistic about our chances. I could forgive and move on in the sense that spiritual writer Stephen Levine described: "It is mercy in action in the same way that compassion is wisdom in action."

I tried to look at the bigger picture. We're all doing our best with the relationship skills we have.

Levine wrote, as he faced a terminal illness, "Forgiveness does not condone unkind actions, but it does embrace the momentary actor whose unskillful ways led to such unskillful conduct."

Would my husband and I ever feel close enough to want to live together again? The answer to that question was unclear as Donald visited for a few days after my treatment to get me over the treacherous hump of wretched side effects. Problems after each infusion varied, with some of them getting worse over time. After getting through my second treatment, with Carla again at my side, I observed the effects, writing, *My head looks threadbare, with pink scalp showing through. After each chemotherapy, my body shuts down tight, skin smooth as glass, each pore shuttered for a storm.*

Casey sent me a message urging me to pray "with your mind already made up. Keep calm and turn poison into medicine." I incorporated an hour of chanting, prayer, and meditation into each day, sometimes with Donald by my side, when he was around.

A box arrived from my Illinois friend, Kiyoko, whose daughter had survived breast cancer. I was surprised to find a bonsai inside, amazed that you could mail a living tree to somebody. I placed the trimmed and stunted umbrella tree on a shelf by the window, its roots tucked into the soil of a shallow rectangular pot, and it reminded me of a journal entry I wrote on an autumn day a year before I had moved to Whidbey. Donald had arrived home at 3:15 a.m. from a music session. We were about as far apart as any couple could be and still live together. No longer willing to sacrifice my growth to a withered, unfulfilling marriage, I wrote, with a little humor:

I'm not a bonsai tree.
Don't contain me.
I need room to grow —
in all directions.
Step away from the clippers!

A few journal pages later, back on Whidbey Island for a six-week visit, I wrote, *How do you find, claim, and develop those parts of yourself that have been marginalized, devalued, and unheard? How do you reclaim your heart?* I then quoted Erica Jong's character, Isadora Wing, in *Fear of Flying*: "A good woman would have given over her life to the care and feeding of her husband's madness. I was not a good woman. I had too many other things to do."

On Whidbey, I had better things to do than fret over my partner's behavior. I was attending workshops, helping Emily wash wool shorn from their sheep, and exploring the island that would become my home.

The little tree from Kiyoko was pretty in a controlled kind of way. It was not my way. I preferred a healthy balance with lots of room to grow. Fertile, fifty-mile-long Whidbey Island was proving to be an appropriate "container" where I was neither lost nor confined, flourishing upward even as my roots extended deep into the soil.

❧

Four days after my chemo treatment, Emily and Alex picked up Donald at the shuttle stop in Clinton. The three of them made supper in our Langley house, with chicken, squash, Romanesco cauliflower, asparagus, and rice. I rested on the sofa, watching the Academy Awards on television. My mouth pain was getting worse, my tongue was not at home in my mouth, and my digestive system was confused. When I felt queasy, I took an anti-nausea prescription and quickly felt better, but the alternating constipation and diarrhea took a toll on my energy. Some side effects had no remedies, or I couldn't tolerate my usual methods of relief, such as minty Tums that now stung my mouth and throat. But supper was custom-made for me, and I ate a bit of everything they cooked.

The next morning, Donald made miso soup with rice for our breakfast, one of my favorites. It was comforting to have him with me. Accustomed to the easy camaraderie I'd found with friends on the island, I looked at my newly arrived husband across the table and initiated a conversation, starting with the dog, to catch up with each other. "How's Cassie been doing?"

"Fine," he said, sipping his coffee.

A few bites later, I asked, "Anything new in the neighborhood?"

He shrugged and shook his head. My efforts to converse fell flat. Anxiety pinched off my esophagus as we sat in stony silence. It was hard to swallow the tofu and wakame seaweed in my soup. The umami deliciousness of the broth was lost on me. While I'd become accustomed to living with a quiet man, I never got used to our sterile, empty mealtimes; I missed the lively dinner discussions our family had when I was growing up. When together, Donald and I seemed to revert to our old patterns, the ones that drove me out of my mind and out of our Illinois house. It was depressing for me, and I didn't want to feel so lonely and shut out again.

Could we have an engaging conversation about something besides my cancer, his music life, or our kids' lives? I searched my mind for common topics of interest, the overlapping spot on the Venn diagram of our two stories, and came up with a quirky one: working with lab rats during college. I asked what he remembered about the white rats at his university in Indiana. I was hoping the question would kickstart a discussion or at least lead to other topics, as friendly conversations tend to do.

"Well," Donald said, "if the newborn rats fell out of their cages and we couldn't determine which cage they came from, we had to put them down the garbage disposal."

"Oh, how sad!" I said, waiting for him to say more. After a silent spell, I spoke again. "What I remember most is taking photos of the Rat Park addiction experiment when I was at Simon Fraser." The results of the research caused a stir at the time because the isolated, caged rats were easily hooked on drugs (offered to them in their water), while those in the stimulating, highly social environment of Rat Park declined the drugs and drank plain water.

"I've been thinking about it," I explained, "because my friend, Pam, posted a link to a new article about it. I find it cool that Bruce Alexander's findings are still relevant." As I thought about the way Dr. Alexander debunked popular theories of addiction forty years ago, my brain sparked and flared. (Maybe I was too nerdy. No wonder I didn't do well with party talk.) The implications of the research were fascinating to me. How I would love to have a partner who'd discuss them with me!

Donald got up from the table to clean the coffeepot, his

blank face confirming I'd lost his attention several sentences back. I tried one more time to connect. "Isn't that interesting?"

"All you do is social media," Donald said in a disparaging tone. When he saw me sit back and widen my eyes at him, he added, with a sour look, "I guess I'm not into rats like you are." Perhaps that was meant to be humorous, but it felt insulting. The miso gruel curdled in my stomach. Having shut down the interaction, he left me sitting at the table, well fed yet still starving.

Actions speak louder than words. Donald had traveled a long way to shepherd me through a health crisis, and I appreciated that. Was I expecting too much from my Japanese American spouse?

I grew up with a set of ideals and expectations about marriage not necessarily shared by my husband. As Jungian psychologist Robert A. Johnson wrote, "In Eastern cultures, like those of India or Japan, we find that married couples love each other with great warmth, often with a stability and devotion that puts us to shame. But their love is not 'romantic love' as we know it."

With our many cultural and personality differences, I wasn't sure "great warmth" was even a possibility for us.

❖

On his last night before returning to our dog and our Illinois home, I felt well enough to go to a bistro in Langley with Donald, Emily, and Alex. We celebrated Emily's birthday coming up and Alex's new general contracting license. (Alex and Emily planned to build a sheep barn, among other things.) Their enthusiasm and happiness were infectious; even Donald, who has a hard time hearing in noisy restaurants, chimed in, saying he'd like to help with projects on the farm.

Then, when I drove my husband to the shuttle for his return trip to Chicago the next day, we had a brief chance to talk in the car. His departures were sometimes the setting for any residual conflicts to come to a head, at least for me. I'd make an effort to be heard before he left, knowing that any disagreement that arose was on a strict time limit, based on the shuttle schedule. Lacking the energy for a fight, I wanted to make my words count while avoiding Donald's retaliatory anger, which was often his first response to my concerns.

A Cleveland man, Matthew Fray, once wrote an illuminating post about ignoring the dishes and losing his wife. It spread online like a tsunami, a wake-up call to unaware spouses and an affirmation of those who'd borne the brunt of the emotional and household work necessary to maintain a marriage and a home. When it came to discussing marital issues, Fray noticed husbands' initial reactions were to judge their wives, making no effort to address their concerns.

Fray said in an interview, "They dispute the facts of the story their partner just told; agree with the facts, but believe their partner is overreacting; or defend their actions by explaining why they did it. In all three cases, his partner's feelings are invalid."

I preferred to forgo those phases of criticizing, lecturing, and yelling by giving Hub a few weeks or, in this case, two months, to consider what I said, let it sink in, and maybe even see my point.

I'd come to believe that my reticent husband had stories about me in his head, based on a different reality than mine. One of the few times we sat down to have a personal discussion, I said I'd like to talk about our assumptions and what's on our minds.

"Where'd you get this idea? From the Internet?" Donald had asked, leaning back in a chair across from me.

"No," I said, "I woke up thinking that we need a reality check now and then. I know you tend to do a lot of thinking in your own head."

With a dose of sarcasm, he said, "Where do you do your thinking?"

"Out loud," I said, aware this was a major difference between us. Then I told him I wasn't sure if I could trust him anymore, and he insisted I could. In turn, he asked me if I first went to Whidbey knowing I wanted to buy a house. I started to explain the complexity of my intentions and motivations, but Donald stepped over to the kitchen and started chopping onions, so I cut it short. "No," I said, "I didn't realize I'd want to move until after I got to know the island."

While my way of thinking out loud may have been annoying to my husband, his unspoken internal process had its downsides too. Maybe we're all constructing scenarios in our minds, which is fine—as long as we allow room for fact-checking. Donald had told me many times, both directly such as at Ten Mile House, and indirectly by ignoring me or pushing me away, that in his view I was a hindrance to his happiness and an obstacle to his freedom and creativity. In contrast, my version of my role in our marriage was that I was committed to uplifting my husband and enhancing his life, not bringing him down or limiting him. Donald's negative attitude toward me seemed cruel. If he didn't like me the way I was, and the more authentic way I now lived, liking the hell out of myself, it was time for a reality check—for both of us. Maybe we weren't meant for each other.

As we sat in the parking lot at Ken's Korner, waiting for the shuttle van, I said, "You know, many people I've met here like me and trust me. Maybe if you got to know me—and not just the wife in your head—you'd like me, too."

The shuttle arrived before Donald could say anything to that. Which was perfect timing.

Food for thought.

14

GOOD COMPANY

*Our most meaningful relationships are often those that
continued beyond the juncture at which
they came closest to ending.*
—CHERYL STRAYED

*M*y husband left at the beginning of March. I wouldn't
see him again till the end of April. I had others, namely
my daughter Stephanie and my friend Amy, lined up to help me
with my next two cancer treatments and their side effects. When
Stephanie completed her work in Hawaii, she came to visit me
before returning to New York City.

Ever since my eldest child made me a mother by being born,
I've adored her. She and her father are both Sagittarians born in
the Year of the Ox, and I haven't a clue what is going on in their
heads half the time, but I know they are both magnificently creative. I was one of those smitten mothers, thinking my child had
artistic talent from a very young age. And I was not wrong; she's
become an artist and artisan, helping to devise such things as a
Times Square attraction with tiny people in scenes from around
the world. Stephanie also has an infinitely kind heart.

Accompanying me to my third chemotherapy treatment,

Steph helped me browse the handmade hats and knitted knockers in the resource room for cancer patients. I chose a brown wool hat to keep my head warm and a knitted knocker to fill my bra after my mastectomy. There were wigs in the resource room too, but I'd already purchased a pixie brunette wig at a shop next to H Mart, with the help of my friend, Raya. After my infusions, Stephanie and I picked up treats at a Seattle bakery and shared them with Emily and Alex when we got back to Whidbey Island.

The next day, while I felt well enough, Stephanie and I walked in Ebey's Reserve, traversing the bluff high above the Salish Sea, past historical markers about early settlers on the island. When we came home, Steph planted daffodil and tulip bulbs in my yard. One afternoon, Stephanie, Emily, and I joined Emily's neighbor, Dynva, and we made bird feeders out of gourds. I painted lotus flowers on mine.

As my appetite waned, Stephanie concocted drinks for me. "Steph," I said, "I can't eat much of anything, but I can still drink your smoothies! In fact, my stomach feels better when I do."

"That's because I put fresh ginger in there along with the apples and kale," she said. "It settles your stomach."

I missed her when she went back to New York.

When Amy arrived from the Midwest a couple weeks later, she had her own place to stay a few doors down from my house. A neighbor needed a house sitter and pet sitter, and when I let Amy know, she volunteered. Good with animals, she often took care of other people's dogs back in Minnesota.

I was surprised to learn Amy's visit to Whidbey Island was her first trip alone outside of her home state. The magnitude of this was not lost on me, and I cherished my lifelong friend being nearby as I went through more health challenges. I warned her that I'd be feeling the w's: weak, weary, wobbly, weepy, and weird. Meanwhile, when I had the energy, I showed her the sights. Our best adventure was a cruise to see gray whales feeding on ghost shrimp along the shores of Whidbey Island and Hat Island. Watching the whales' backs curving above the water and then flowing back down again was so mesmerizing, I forgot all about cancer. Amy stood on the deck watching them with binoculars long after I'd gone inside the cabin to get out of the wind.

When Amy accompanied me to chemotherapy, she was curious about my treatments. As the oncology nurse hung my IV bag, Amy asked, "What do the chemotherapy drugs do?"

The nurse paused to think and I, being the smart-ass that I am, jumped in and said, "They're poisons they give me to save my life."

The nurse and I shared a look, which I took as an agreement not to sugarcoat the matter. Then she nodded and started the infusion.

"That's right," was all she said.

❃.

When Donald returned to Whidbey at the end of April, we were more mellow with each other. Cognitive side effects hit me harder than usual, so I could hardly think. My eyes were jittery, and my head seemed full of pebbles. When I felt a bit better, Donald took me to the river town of La Connor on the mainland. We ate at Calico Cupboard Cafe and browsed the shops and galleries, marveling that we'd found free parking in the popular tourist destination. We stopped to see Emily on the way home, just enjoying the simple things couples do together.

Was my husband's cynical attitude toward me completely

gone? It was hard to tell. Donald never mentioned a conscious change in his thinking or behavior, but he seemed to have taken the hint to see me in a new light and consider me a valued partner and human being rather than as an obstacle to be kicked aside.

For my part, I remembered how preoccupied I'd been with raising our children and later, with the ramifications of my mother's death in 2010 and the stress of dealing with family issues regarding her estate, all of which may have taken a toll on our marriage. Was that lack of attention the reason Donald became so devoted to playing guitar? Even if that was the case, and knowing music was his chosen art form, I didn't think it should be a higher priority than our marriage. Author and farmer Wendell Berry advised writers, musicians, and other artists to get their priorities in order. Yes, there are times to focus on your art. "But," he said, "if you have a marriage and a family and a farm, you're just going to find that you can't always put your art first, and moreover that you shouldn't. There are a number of things more important than your art."

The way Donald was taking care of me during his visit gave me a glimmer of hope that I was a priority, and that maybe we could maintain our marriage without imploding.

I also tried to acknowledge our cultural differences and take them into account when assessing our situation. Donald and his brother, while Americanized to a great extent, were surrounded by Japanese influences as they grew up. Their mother, Lily, was born in Seattle but lived in Japan for much of her youth and went to high school there. Back in the United States, she was released from her internment camp during WWII so she could teach Japanese to military intelligence officers who would be interrogating prisoners. (She was given a medal, posthumously, for her service.) For a while, Lily's sister, Miyeko, who preferred to speak Japanese, lived with their family. Asian culture was a constant presence in the Terao household and no doubt had an effect on my husband.

Reading *Polite Lies: On Being a Woman Caught between Cultures* by Kyoko Mori helped me understand societal pressures in Japan. "My mother spent most of her adult life trying to live a polite lie of a stable and harmonious marriage," she wrote.

In Mori's essays, I recognized familiar issues in her description of marriages observed in Japan before she moved to the Midwest. "We grew up watching our mothers working hard as housekeepers, silent hostesses, and errand-women for our fathers, who never thanked their wives except by a begrudging nod or barely audible grunt."

I'd received my share of grudging communication—when I could get any response at all.

In contrast with her American friends, Mori noted, "None of my Japanese friends have ever talked about the great conversations they have with their husbands, the emotional support they get from them in times of trouble, or even the fun they have together on trips."

Those were missing pieces for me, too. I wanted emotional rapport, amiable conversation, and a marriage based on an appreciation of each other and our life together. My expectations were derived from relationships I'd witnessed while growing up, especially my parents' marriage, along with Western notions of romance and compatibility. I did not want to live a "polite lie" with Donald.

Who knows how many have lost their way by living a lie? Pretense is detrimental to our health, as I discovered when I tried to be someone I'm not.

As Mrs. Masuda told me, "Be Barbara or you're going to explode." (Maybe cancer was the explosion, or at least its smolder-
ing fuse, giving me warning.)

Both my husband and I were breaking though illusions and
old notions of who we could be. As I considered his background,
raised by second-generation Japanese Americans, I could see
that he was trying in his own way to keep our marriage together.
I was relieved that, during Donald's April visit, there was a shift
toward harmony as we operated more as friends than enemies.

Spring arrived earlier in Washington than in Illinois. Trees
blossomed by the end of February. Hope emerged from the wet
fog of winter. When I took Donald to the shuttle, we were in a
pleasant, joking mood and he admitted he was starting to prefer
the mild temperatures of the Pacific Northwest over the ex-
tremes of the Midwest.

❀

By the fifth cycle of treatment, I was starting to get itchy welts
along my backside, which I finally figured out were hives. I'd
never had hives before. Wishing to spare my body, I prayed for
an end to chemo *and* for victory over cancer. When Carla and I
went for my sixth and final chemo cycle, I noticed the toll-taker
at the ferry take a second glance at me as I showed her my medical pass. I probably looked healthy to her. I briefly considered
pulling off my auburn wig to show my bald head and prove my
legitimacy, but she simply directed us to the front of the line.

When we arrived at my HMO in Seattle, I met with Dr. Panjwani, the oncologist on duty. My white blood cells had returned
to a healthy level, as usual, but the hives concerned her. "Barbara,
we don't want you having hives. This is likely an allergic reaction

to your chemotherapy drugs." Dr. Panjwani, who spoke with an Indian lilt in her voice, swiveled to her computer screen. "Your MRI results look good, so we know your treatments are working. Your tumors are shrinking. I also see you've been having difficulty with side effects."

I clutched my hands together at the mention of side effects. "That's true," I said, my eyes misting over. "It's been really tough."

"Well," Dr. Panjwani said, turning to me, "you've finished five cycles of chemotherapy. Enough. Let us declare victory at this time."

I was in rapture to hear the oncologist echo the word *victory*—and answer my prayer for an end to chemo. Though the targeted therapy of Herceptin would continue every three weeks, I was confident I could handle its mild side effects. Nodding my head, I said, "Yes, yes, that would be great." I floated out of the room, as relieved as though I'd escaped the gallows. After receiving my ongoing infusion of Herceptin and my final infusion of Perjeta, Carla and I still had time to go out for lunch.

When I called Donald with the good news that I was done with Taxotere and carboplatin, he congratulated me. "So, you're done with the worst of it? That's great!"

Then he asked if he should still come for his next visit, since I wouldn't need his help managing side effects. I understood that to be Donald's way of feeling out the situation. The ball was in my court to invite or uninvite him. Was he still welcome? It occurred to me that I'd come to value our time together on the island, as well as our family time with Emily and Alex.

"Sure," I said. "We can do fun stuff for a change. And Alex could use your help on the farm."

Though my chemotherapy was technically over, the nurses

did not invite me to ring a bell or mark the occasion in any way. As a fan of celebratory rituals, I hoped I would have a chance to do so seven months later, at the end of my Herceptin infusions.

❦

When that day in December arrived, Emily and I awaited some acknowledgment that the long ordeal was over, but no such gesture was forthcoming. (Since then, I've learned that hearing the victory bell is not a happy moment for patients with metastatic cancer who receive chemotherapy on a long-term basis. There is no end of treatment in sight for them. So maybe it's just as well I did not have that opportunity.)

I gave my attendant for the day a thank-you note and a gift bag of candy canes and chocolate treats to share with the other nurses. She disappeared into their break room and returned to where my daughter and I stood and, looking apologetic, handed me a coffee mug. A white ceramic mug. I considered refusing the random gift. I didn't need a mug, and I'd obviously put her on the spot. *But* I really wanted a marker of this moment, so I said thank you and accepted it. I would find a way to ring a bell, in a big way, eventually.

15

THE WONDER OF WOMEN

I sing the body electric.
—WALT WHITMAN

The next step in my treatment was removal of my right breast. In June, I prepared for surgery with one big concern on my mind: I didn't want a tube down my throat as is standard procedure. Sure, I wanted anesthesia so I'd be knocked out during the amputation, but I didn't want a big honking hose jammed in my throat, bruising my tender tissue as happened in 2012. After my abdominal surgery for endometriosis, I was in bed for a week, taking tiny sips of water in hopes the liquid would slip past the big slug of swollen uvula lying on my tongue. I couldn't speak. I could hardly breathe.

I described that experience to my surgeon, Dr. Starr. Though she understood my objection to intubation, she didn't give me much hope of avoiding it.

"You'll have to talk with the anesthesiologist because that's how they manage your breathing while you're unconscious," she said.

I told her I would chant *Nam-myoho-renge-kyo* for the best outcome.

I wanted the surgery to be short and simple and asked my

medical oncologist, Dr. Chisolm, if I could skip the sentinel node biopsy. I didn't believe it was necessary to check beyond my breast for malignant cells. Perhaps due to his inexperience as an oncologist, he agreed. It was one of the few times he did not insist on "standard procedure."

After my appointment with Dr. Starr, I called the anesthesiology department. The doctor who called me back said, predictably, "That's the standard of care. Blah, blah, blah, must do tube down throat."

I was my only advocate; I'd never known my husband to ever question a doctor's decision, and I didn't want to put my children in the position of confronting my caregivers. I was on my own and did my best to make good decisions and stick up for myself. But the weight of the HMO's bureaucracy was too much to bear. I saw no way to talk the doctors out of the dreaded tube.

On the day of my surgery, with a hefty, gray-haired anesthesiologist by my gurney in the hall, I tried one more time to make my case. We were stuck in limbo between waiting room and operating room for a minute while I negotiated with him. "I'm worried about my uvula swelling again. Even now, it's still a little enlarged from my surgery five years ago. If you must use a tube, could you use a smaller one, like kid-size?"

I saw Dr. Starr and the nurse anesthetist, Christina, coming around the corner and cast them a pleading look from my prone position on the gurney.

Christina stepped forward, as if she'd just thought of something. "What if we give her propofol intravenously and use a regional anesthetic on her chest?" she said to the anesthesiologist while looking straight at me. "Then she wouldn't have to be intubated."

I nodded at her, smiling broadly enough to light up the dim

hallway, signaling my gratitude for her suggestion. Dr. Starr was nodding, too, but thoughtfully, as if this was an unusual but reasonable idea.

The gray-haired doctor grumbled something about Christina's suggestion "possibly" being a viable option. Not wanting to aggravate him, I said as diplomatically as I could, "I'd be okay with that option." An agreement was reached, and the anesthesiologist, who had, in my view, become extraneous, left me to the two brilliant women who took my concerns to heart.

In the operating room, I felt a burning sensation as drugs flowed through an IV in my hand. I imagined a pink cloud of protection around me as I slipped out of consciousness. (Dr. Starr later told me I kept talking under sedation and said my Buddhist prayers.) Next thing I knew I was in the recovery room, where I was to spend the night. The simple mastectomy, with no lymph nodes removed, was complete. Donald was sitting next to my bed as a nurse instructed him in my post-surgical care. When the nurse, Nell, saw I was alert, she asked if I wanted something to eat. I noticed that I felt surprisingly well. Because I'd avoided general anesthesia, I had no nausea, headache, or swollen throat.

"Yes, please," I said, "I am kind of hungry." As I ate my yogurt and apple, Donald told me goofy things I'd said while coming out of sedation. As I was wheeled toward the recovery room, I apparently saw Donald in the hall and waved to him, saying, "Give me a kiss!" I couldn't remember any of that.

When Nell returned to the room, she brought me more food—a salad with fresh mozzarella balls, which I devoured with gusto. Then she walked with me down the hall of the HMO to evaluate my mobility.

"Well, Barbara," she said, "you're supposed to stay overnight, but it's not required. Would you like to go home?"

Yes, I liked that idea. Dr. Starr came by and gave her approval, and I was released into Donald's care.

We didn't have a chance to acknowledge Father's Day when Donald arrived the previous Sunday, so we celebrated on Tuesday, the day after my surgery. While I rested in the living room, Emily and Alex prepared Chinese dumplings and other delicacies from scratch. I wore a turban over my paltry bit of hair that was growing back and a loose button-up shirt over my bandage. A rubber tube ran under my skin from sternum to armpit, carrying beet-red fluids from the mastectomy site to a bulb under my arm, which Donald drained and measured several times a day. Moving slowly and carefully, I was able to participate in our festive dinner, which lasted late into the night.

Three days later, Donald took me to my HMO and Dr. Starr removed the drainage tube. "Just when you're starting to get mad at me, it will be over," she said, as she thrust her hand away from my chest as if pulling the cord of an outboard motor. The sensation of the removal was weird but not painful.

The next day, free of bandages and drainage paraphernalia, I felt ready to take a full shower. I delighted in returning to this sign of normalcy, humming as I soaped up my hands and slid them over my wet torso. I lifted my left breast to clean under it and then, out of habit, tried to do the same on the right. With no speedbump of tissue there to stop it, my soapy hand just kept going up my smooth, flat torso. I whacked myself under the chin and, a little dazed, realized my error. Was it comedy or tragedy? I burst into laughter, not tears, glad I still had my sense of humor. I did not mourn the loss of my right breast, my bosom buddy gone rogue. I did not grieve the mastectomy because it was part of saving my life. I could try to embrace the imperfection, impermanence, and asymmetry that the Japanese call *wabi sabi*, which is said to have its own kind of beauty. Appreciating what is broken or unexpected is a lesson in itself.

My nurse friend, Jill, came by the cottage to check on me. She scolded me at first for having removed my bandage, but when she inspected my scar, she changed her mind.

"It looks good, Barbara! You're healing well."

I gave Jill a big smile. "I'm glad you say so, because I want to go to the movies with you tonight," I told her. "The *Wonder Woman* movie is playing at the Clyde, and she's my inspiration to get through all this crap. Donald is not interested, so I'm going with Raya and Carla. Want to come with us?" Jill gave me a skeptical look as I led her into my closet. "Here, help me put on my leggings and tank top. I want to dress up for tonight." Though hardly able to lift my right arm, I wiggled into my blue shirt with Jill's help. Encircling my fuzzy head, I sported a sparkly red headband. Wide bracelets wrapped my wrists, presumably to channel lightning and deflect bullets like the bands worn by my Amazonian superhero.

Carla and Raya came by my cottage with their own sparkly accessories. The four of us went to the theater, walking in like Amazon queens. The little movie house was packed, and enthusiasm was high. We watched Wonder Woman (played by Gal Gadot) evolve on the screen, and she was spectacular. After being flattened by cancer treatments, it was invigorating to see strong female characters and cheer them on. I thought of the story of female warriors who removed their right breasts so they could pull back their bows unimpeded. Though no such body alteration was depicted in the archery scenes of the film, I felt a sisterhood with the mythic women.

On the way out, Lynn, the owner of the theater, greeted me and asked, "Did I hear Carla say you'll have a mastectomy soon?"

"Actually, I had it last Monday," I said.

Lynn tilted her head and said, "Five days ago?" like I must be joking.

I, too, was surprised that I was out with friends so soon after surgery. "Yeah, it may seem hard to believe, but I had a good surgeon and good care," I said, pointing to the three women with me. "And seeing this movie is part of my recovery!" Lynn wished me well and Jill drove me home. The next day, Donald departed, and my sister, Joan, arrived to fatten me up with tasty pancakes and curries.

Joan and I took a walk along Bowman Bay in Deception Pass State Park. When we came upon a hollow stump of a Douglas fir about my height, I climbed inside and hunkered down. I felt cozy and content leaning on the soft, crumbly wood, and I breathed in the fragrance of the old tree as if it were medicine.

My sister snapped a picture, saying, "The tree-hugger gets a tree hug!" Indeed, I felt embraced.

16

THANKS FOR THE MAMMARIES

For women, tears are the beginning of the initiation into the Scar Clan, that timeless tribe of women of all colors, all nations, all languages, who down through the ages have lived through a great something, and yet who stood proud.
—CLARISSA PINKOLA ESTÉS

omen's breasts receive a great deal of attention in Western culture, some welcome and some not. They are a significant part of our identities, so it's long been assumed that anyone losing a breast would opt to create a new one by any means necessary. A typical comment to women facing mastectomies is, "Lucky you! You get a boob job for free." It was only recently that remaining flat-chested after surgery became a popular option. Women were, and sometimes still are, pushed into plastic surgery to create artificial breasts after mastectomies. For some doctors, it seemed unthinkable for a woman to choose otherwise. Fortunately, most breast cancer surgeries are covered by insurance, including breast reconstruction, if that option is selected, or no reconstruction. And, of course, some women only need lumpectomies and can keep most of their breasts.

My medical circumstances had me contemplating my

anatomy in new ways. Ever since I was diagnosed with tumors in my right breast, I was ready and willing to have that one removed. I was anxious for the surgeon to take out all the cancer, the sooner the better. It was a harder decision whether to keep my left breast or have it removed along with the cancerous one. Some women have genetic profiles suggesting a need for prophylactic surgery of that type. Since I'd never had genetic testing, I didn't think that applied to me.

When I asked my husband if he had any feelings or opinions regarding my decision, he said, "It's up to you, so whatever you want to do is okay with me." He put his arms around me and said, "You're still my wife."

Oncologist Susan Love found that most partners of breast cancer patients are "more concerned with the women's health than their appearance," which was the case with my husband.

I let myself daydream of life after a double mastectomy, considering the advantages of going completely flat, taking me back to my youth, running around with no need for a bra. The freedom in that! No cleavage to show or not show. No tender flesh moving uncomfortably on a horseback ride or getting in the way of a yoga twist. Throw on underpants, jeans, and a T-shirt and go about my day. Yet I had to ask myself if there were any clinical reasons to amputate the healthy breast. It was deemed cancer free, so any medical arguments for removal were hypothetical. Sometimes a remaining breast develops cancer later in life. More disturbing, cancer is sometimes found in a seemingly healthy breast that is removed during a double mastectomy because tests are not perfect. Could my mammogram, ultrasounds, and MRI have missed something? I had to weigh that possibility.

Though it was hard to be completely certain, I chose to believe the test results showing that my left side was fine. "If it ain't broke, don't fix it," as my dad used to say. I didn't want to have more surgery than was required for my survival. Neither a left mastectomy nor reconstruction was necessary to keep me alive. I didn't have the heart to have a double mastectomy and discard a part of my body that had done nothing to offend and had done much to enhance my life and feed my children. So I had a single.

Sometimes it's hard to imagine our bodies without our mammary glands. Chemotherapy and surgery for breast cancer often mean that we lose two of our main attractions, our hair and our breasts. Even our eyelashes disappear! How do you dress up for a date after that? We may feel damaged, broken, or diminished. Yet it can be a chance to know ourselves laid bare, minus our shields and adornments. Perhaps it's when we're broken that we most clearly see our true nature in its wholeness.

What is required of us to go forward? Some people venture into new territory, as Diana Lindsay and her husband did by founding Healing Circles because of her cancer diagnosis. A striking example of a new mindset was that of Anita Moorjani in her 2012 book, *Dying to Be Me: My Journey from Cancer, to Near Death, to True Healing,* often brought up in online breast cancer sites I followed. Describing how she flipped her perspective, Moorjani wrote about how she had looked outside herself for answers. She relied on her doctors to make decisions for her, rarely expressing herself, and finally noticed, "I only ended up feeling even more adrift because I was giving my own power away again and again. I found that having an inside-out view means being able to fully trust my inner guidance." Moorjani learned to listen to her own mind, body, and spirit, along with listening to her doctors. After four years of metastatic cancer, her tumors disappeared, and she recovered her health.

Oncologist M. Laura Nasi wrote in her book, *Cancer As a*

Wake-Up Call: An Oncologist's Integrative Approach to What You Can Do to Become Whole Again, "A disease might be the soul making its voice heard. . . . When we try to fit into the mold of life as others and our conditioning tell us it should be, we ignore or repress parts of ourselves, and eventually we'll get sick."

If we've been presenting ourselves as an invulnerable rock, or on the other extreme as an ever-accommodating caregiver, cancer blows our facades to smithereens. We *are* vulnerable, and we *do* need others to care for us sometimes. Daring to be authentic, we touch base with our deeper self and find a jewel to be treasured and protected. Life coach Martha Beck dealt with chronic, painful health problems for years and felt frustrated by her limitations until she had an epiphany while visiting Londolozi Game Reserve in South Africa. Considering her body's challenges with appreciation for her true nature and its interconnection with all beings, she realized, "Physical existence has taught me things through pain that enhance my capacity for joy." She advises, for herself and for all of us, "Your job, now and for the rest of your life, is to heal that true nature and let it thrive."

I've sought reminders of my true nature from such role models of empowerment, something other than the image of Agatha, considered by some to be the patron saint of breast cancer, whose breasts were torn off as a form of medieval torture. On a mystical level, the Indian deity Kali, described by Mirabai Starr as "relentless in her love and spiritual badassness," carries a sword that cuts through illusions. Saraswati, the goddess of creativity, speaks in lyrics that ring true as a bell. I wanted more of these shimmering female archetypes, and I wished for recognizable representations of cancer survivors to honor our scarred bodies.

Where are the images of surgery survivors and one-mammary mermaids, the reconfigured bodies that empower? Let's milk the myths of warrior women, such as the one-breasted Amazons. As the story goes, they removed their right breasts to be better archers. Pulling their bowstrings taut against their smooth chests, they released the string with full freedom of intent into the world with no impediments. Like Amazon warriors, we can be empowered rather than diminished, with clarity of our intentions. We dare to speak our minds and tell our stories. The fear that rides along as cancer's sidekick is felled by those arrows, those truths. Our strength.

Some mastectomy survivors, such as the women in the Flat & Fabulous online group, post pictures of their half-flat or fully flat chests. Some bare chests are etched with healed incisions while others have colorful tattoos dancing across their scar lines. Our sex appeal may seem momentarily dimmed, but our inner light is not. Even reconfigured, we are fabulous.

I accepted the fact that my treasured chest would never be the same, and I had no interest in plastic surgery to make a new boob. Inspired by other cancer survivors who've gone flat, I chose to get a removable one instead. I was not self-conscious to be lopsided around friends and family, but I imagined occasions when I'd rather avoid drawing stares of strangers to my body. If I wanted to look symmetrical, I needed more than the knitted knocker I picked up at the Cancer Resource Room. I needed a prosthesis.

Emily and I went on a mission. Well, two missions. She needed footwear, not having shopped for shoes in three years, and I needed a right breast, having been without one for several weeks. I was in search of a fake boob to balance out my chest on those rare occasions when I wanted to dress up or wear form-fitting clothes. My oncologist recommended Nordstrom department store as the closest place to fill my prescription for a new body part. Not advertised to shoppers, the store's Breast Prosthesis Program was tucked away in the lingerie department. There, women dealing with breast cancer have a more pampered and personalized experience than in a clinic or medical supply store, leaving with their choice of prostheses and brassieres, all covered by insurance.

Living on an island in Puget Sound, we had to go to the other side, as islanders say, to find any such thing as a mall. My daughter came over early, straight from her farm chores. It only took me a few minutes to brush my teeth, comb my short hair, and grab a jacket. Then we drove to the terminal where the green-and-white ferry waited to take us across the water.

I still had my medical pass. Starting to feel halfway normal, I wondered if my condition justified special treatment. But then I reminded myself, *This is not a mere pleasure trip. I have an appointment to be fitted with a prosthetic breast because my real one was going to kill me.* The gracious fellow at the tollbooth accepted my medical status, sending us to loaders who gave us a prime place onboard with a view of the sea. As always, my eyes blurred with tears of gratitude for the kindness of hearts and the grace of gulls. The fifteen-minute trip was a chance to behold the beauty of sun on water and tall trees along the shores, the rustic beauty of the place where we lived.

Emily worked multiple jobs, so I didn't get to see her very often. I was a little giddy to have a mother-daughter outing, a nod to the normal after a distinctly abnormal—and grueling— eight months of chemotherapy, targeted therapy, and surgery. We arrived at the store as it opened for the day.

"Do you want me to walk you to your appointment?" Emily asked.

"Yes, please, so I don't seem like some kind of sad cancer lady," I said with an exaggerated frowny face. Then I brightened into a smile. "I'm just a mom out shopping with her daughter!"

My insurance covered, as "medical equipment," one artificial breast and two mastectomy bras. A salesclerk named Annabelle took me into a posh, carpeted dressing room and brought me a series of artificial breasts that looked and felt like chicken cutlets. I chose the one that felt the least clammy and tried it on with bras that had pockets to hold it in place. There was a weight to the prosthesis, which was intentional for the sake of posture and balance, replacing the pound and a half of my missing breast. No longer cold and clammy when tucked into its pocket, the prosthesis was comfortable enough to forget I was wearing it.

I twisted, turned, and leaned over to make sure the new breast stayed in place in the mastectomy bra. Then I put my shirt on and buttoned it up, peering at myself in the mirror to check out my appearance. I looked symmetrical and very much like my old self.

I took off the new gear, got dressed in one of the stretchy bras I'd been wearing since I'd healed from surgery, and went to check out. Along with the cutlet, I got an all-purpose beige bra and a frilly white one, for a touch of femininity. I figured, *Hey, I'm still me! A girl wants a little lace, even if she's flat as a pancake.* Annabelle put my bras and boxed prosthesis in a paper shopping bag, and I went to find Emily.

We met up among the lingerie and made a beeline for the shoes. Nordstrom's was having their anniversary sale, and the place was buzzing. I apprehended a blond blur of a salesperson long enough for him to say his name was Blake and he'd be "right back" to help us. Though Blake was assisting several customers at once, he managed to bring my daughter a raft of styles, chatting with us all the while. He had his own sense of style: button-up shirt, skinny tie, and a bit of glittery white makeup on his cheekbones. It suited him.

After a quick assessment of Emily's plaid shirt, jeans, and worn-out shoes, Blake took on her case as if doing a makeover. He brought her black shoes with pretty ties around the ankles and had her stand in front of a full-length mirror to admire them. Not content to stop there, Blake recommended she put up her long, thick hair in "a messy bun" and wear a white T-shirt. Oh, and skinny black jeans too.

"There are black jeans on sale upstairs with rips already in them!" he added with excitement.

My daughter informed him she made her own rips working on the farm. But we bought the slinky black shoes, along with sandals and walking shoes. With her full shopping bag, Emily and I headed to the exit, and as we got to the door, I realized something was missing. *Where is my shopping bag?* The realization sunk in, giving me a sick feeling in my stomach. I grabbed my daughter's elbow. "Em, wait! I've lost my boob!"

We rushed back to the place where Emily tried on shoes. Nothing. "Blake," I cried when I caught sight of him in the crowd. "I've left my shopping bag somewhere!"

With his astonishing alacrity, Blake scanned the shoe department and located my bag; it was sitting on the sales counter where we paid for the shoes. Handing it to me, he peered with curiosity at the box inside. "That looks interesting! What is it?"

"A fake boob," I said with a wry smile, expecting embarrassment or sympathy on his part.

He clapped his hands with delight and said, "I want one!" Then he added, "No, I want two."

I laughed, though I couldn't help pointing out, "You don't want to get them the way I got mine."

"Well, no," Blake admitted.

I patted his thin shoulder, still laughing. *No sad cancer lady here.* "Thank you, Blake," I said, and, with a wave of his hand, he was off to renovate his next customer.

ME AND THE MOUNTAIN

*Tragedy and trauma are not guarantees for a
transformational spiritual experience, true, but they are
opportunities. They are invitations to sit in the fire and
allow it to transfigure us.*
—MIRABAI STARR

*I*n the middle of August, I took an afternoon ferry to the mainland and drove toward the Cascade Mountains. After passing through the hands of so many doctors and nurses, I wanted to be alone in nature so I could be at home with myself again. Glimpsing Mount Rainier in the distance, the highest peak in Washington, I greeted the volcanic, snow-capped mountain. *I'm coming, Takhoma. I'm still here, still alive! I'm coming to celebrate.*

I spent the night in room 1013 at The Guest House in the town of Enumclaw. The next morning, I drove to Alpine Inn to stay near Mount Rainier National Park and was assigned room 213. The two thirteens in a row made me uneasy as I remembered the unlucky signs and symbols popping up before my breast cancer diagnosis. I pushed my superstitions aside and drove to Sunrise Visitor Center in the national park. At six thousand feet, I wasn't even halfway up Mount Rainier, but it was close enough to meet face-to-face with the glaciated elder.

Alpine hiking is good physical exercise, a mighty challenge for almost anybody. Mountaineer Edmund Hillary implied its transformative benefits when he said, "It's not the mountain we conquer, but ourselves." Personally, I had no goals beyond reaching a wildflower meadow above the tree line. Rather than the fizz of champagne, I would savor my survival with the melody of a mountain stream and the staccato chatting of Douglas squirrels. Mount Rainier, long known as Takhoma (and other names) by Indigenous people, was a cathedral where I could cast my prayers, alive in the glory of its presence. As naturalist John Muir said, "Going to the mountains is going home."

At that altitude, spring wildflowers were still blooming. I walked among pasqueflowers in a green meadow, breathing the cool mountain air. *Thank you for this beauty. Thank you for my life.* I remembered the peace of my favorite Minnesota meadow, the tall grass and wildflowers giving me sanctuary and keeping me company. I was alone, but not lonely. Perhaps along with forest bathing (*shinrin yoku*), we benefit from grass bathing or even mountain bathing! All I know is that I was bewildered by people, not wilderness. I returned to myself in the presence of nature.

For a while, I sat at a scenic picnic table, its wood and I soaking up the sun, with nowhere I'd rather be. With my heart brimmed full of Mount Rainier, it was as poet Li Po said, "We sit together, the mountain and me, until only the mountain remains."

Clarity can come from facing suffering and our own mortality. Even as illness shuts us down, something in us wakes up, reminding us that a lifespan is finite. Nature, friends, and family are seen in a more poignant new light, and we may ask, as did poet Mary Oliver, what are we doing with our "one wild and precious life?"

Driving down from Sunrise, I pulled over by the White River, getting out of my car to explore. The sky was blue, and the river was churned white with glacial run-off, tumbling wild and free. *There are lessons here,* I felt, lingering as the sound of water washed over me. What might I heal in the river's presence? Memories bobbed up in my consciousness: chemotherapy knocking me down, and then my struggles to get back up; feeling forsaken in the maze of my HMO; my husband and I almost giving up on our relationship. As I started to cry, I clambered over the rocky riverbank. There, I sat and let my feelings come up with no critiques or limits, knowing this was why I needed to be alone on this trip, with total freedom to be me. The river was both angel and forgiver, blessing and releasing me.

As did author David James Duncan while observing salmon, I "thanked the prayer wheels that rivers are." Rivers run, prayers rise, and I evolve. Dysfunctional stress may have degraded my health, allowing cancer to take hold, but stress isn't always corrosive. My struggles in dealing with cancer and other problems made me tougher, wiser, and more compassionate. Health psychologist Kelly McGonigal wrote in her book, *The Upside of Stress: Why Stress Is Good for You, and How to Get Good at It,* "Stress is more likely to be harmful when three things are true: 1. You feel inadequate to it; 2. It isolates you from others; and 3. It feels utterly meaningless and against your will." When I was first diagnosed, I did feel inadequate in facing my troubles. But on Whidbey, I never felt isolated. Applying my spiritual practices, I turned poison into medicine and found (or created) meaning.

Immersing my cupped hands in the cold water, I splashed

my face and neck as both cleansing and christening. Letting the breeze dry my cheeks, I thought, *Don't get stuck on disappointments, depression, or despair. Be like the flowing river.* As Francis Weller wrote in *The Wild Edge of Sorrow: Rituals of Renewal and the Sacred Work of Grief,* "When we are in touch with all of our emotions, we are more verb than noun, more a movement than a thing. . . . Grief is part of the dance."

Borrowing the momentum of the rushing water, I cast away old pain, old roles, and old stories on its currents. I granted grace to others as well as myself, forgiving my mistakes, naiveté, and even my succumbing to cancer. I was not the same person I once was. Two months past my mastectomy, with a pink scar on my chest, it was time to let go of the pre-cancer me, the Dilly/Babbit of my youth, and "be Barbara" as Mrs. Masuda advised.

As for the Wolf Spirit name given to me by Ed McGaa, it was part of me now. Just as I knew the mountain's power when I gazed up to its peak, I knew spirit power when I looked within. I perceived my animal ally as a calm presence, sometimes in the background and sometimes warm by my side. After facing the random and wily ways of disease, I needed to connect with both wolf and mountain to reclaim my spirit, my life, and my peace of mind.

Back in my cozy, Bavarian-style room on Crystal Mountain, I sat in a brown leather chair and wrote in my journal, *I am amazed I can be so happy. I love me, I love life. I have beloved family and friends. I have become a more giving and forgiving person. I have strength and wisdom and a voice. I make my own path, not tied to childhood legacies. I make way for the new.*

Of course, I hoped "the new" meant better health and complete recovery from side effects. I wanted to go forward free and clear of cancer, but my celebratory mood was tempered by caution. I thought of myself as someone who relied on science more than superstition, but those room numbers ending in thirteen were hanging around, planted in the worry box of my brain. I felt like I was done with cancer, but was cancer done with me?

18

PARALLEL PLAY HOUSE

It's the secret of a happy marriage to have different interests.
—QUEEN ELIZABETH II

O ne thing I could do to stay healthy was to reduce the amount of estrogen in my system. (Even when in menopause, as I was, our bodies continue to produce hormones.) My breast cancer was estrogen positive, meaning estrogen promoted its tumors. I was supposed to take a daily pill of Arimidex, an aromatase inhibitor that minimizes estrogen, to prevent the recurrence of cancer. My doctor told me, "Women hate aromatase inhibitors and their side effects." He also said, "With less estrogen, you'll be subject to mood changes, hot flashes, and bone thinning." There were other issues too. A neighbor told me she quit the medication when joint pain became so severe she couldn't function. She'd rather risk cancer than be debilitated.

Their warnings confirmed what I'd been reading about side effects of estrogen blockers, so I started my prescription with trepidation. As I expected, I started feeling angry and impatient, as if I was about to explode. It was like going through menopause again. But this time it only lasted about a week, so I continued taking the Arimidex.

Other than my pill every day and my regular infusions of

Herceptin, a targeted therapy less intense than chemotherapy, my routines seemed to be returning to a post-cancer normal. How serene it was in my little Langley cottage! Yet, after less than two years there, I was thinking of house hunting again, mainly for the happy reason that more family members were coming our way! Stephanie and her husband, John, planned to move from New York City to Whidbey Island. And of course, Emily and Alex were already nearby. For family gatherings, I imagined Donald would be spending more time with us too. We needed a place to accommodate all six of us for holidays and our Second Sunday Suppers.

What would it be like if Donald chose to be with us more often? Would he and I drift back into our old ways, forming separate camps in the same household, physically nearby and emotionally distant? Had our behavior changed or only our expectations of each other? On my part, I no longer wasted time wishing for our metamorphoses into matching butterflies, only a clearer line between our respective cocoons, with friendly flurries of togetherness.

Like toddlers, my husband and I got along best when engaged in what psychologists call parallel play, meaning we liked to be near each other in the same general area, with each of us doing our own thing. (This was more his preference than mine.) If we were to live together again, we'd need separate spaces for our cherished activities, a studio for Donald to play music and a study for me to write.

On the downside, having a man cave, my husband might hole up in it indefinitely. In her book, *Introverts in Love: The Quiet Way to Happily Ever After*, Sophia Dembling cautioned, "The independence of introverts can backfire if you both become so independent that you start running on parallel tracks, spending much of your time pursuing individual interests and fun, and letting togetherness take a back seat."

I was the one to initiate most of our opportunities to socialize, like going out for a dinner date or meeting up with other people. Apparently, homebodies often ride the energy of their extrovert partners, relying on and even admiring their sociability. One introvert told Dembling he liked his wife's easy connections with others, saying she could "make friends with a rock." That sounded like me because I made friends with people, animals, trees, and yes, even rocks! Maybe that was one of my roles in our marriage, one of the ways we balanced each other out. My quiet husband was less likely to seek out companionship or new experiences, satisfied with his path running parallel to mine.

I was ready to take on the challenge of finding a home on Whidbey Island that suited both our personalities. The other reason for moving was a weird one. My hearing was becoming more and more sensitive to the point where I was disturbed by every little whisper in the world around me. The less sleep I got, the more I became an acoustic detective. My first case was hunting down the root of the racket below my bedroom window. I'd be slumbering away, lying peacefully under my light-blue quilt, and become gradually aware of an intrusive noise. At first, when the noise stopped, I'd go back to sleep. But after a few disruptive nights, I wanted to find out what the noise was, so I got up and went outside in the dark. Looking around with a flashlight, I traced the intermittent grinding to something called a macerator pump on the side of my house. When I asked my home's builder to come check it out with me the next day, he explained that Langley required the sludge-grinding pump as part of the sewer system, and he agreed it was louder than most. He adjusted it, which helped some.

Then it was the energy recovery ventilator, an integral part of my green-built home, that bothered me. I decided to leave its fan on as white noise to try to cover up other sounds, but it didn't help, so I turned it off altogether. In his Evanston music studio, Donald had had carpet on the walls, and I thought that might be a good idea for my bedroom. The cacophony of small sounds, unnoticeable just a few weeks ago, was now intolerable to me. It wasn't ninety decibels of roar; it was more like thirty decibels of mice squeaking and nibbling on my toes—not as loud as a tiger, but impossible to ignore. Ears are part of our nervous system—always on, always ready to alert us to danger. When roused from sleep by sound waves, stress hormones rush in and blood pressure rises. Waking several times a night was no doubt undermining my health and lowering my immune function, along with disturbing my tranquility.

I asked my oncology team at my HMO if they'd heard of other cancer patients with super-acute hearing, perhaps due to the contrast agent, gadolinium, used for MRIs. Gadolinium is known to linger in the brain. Or could it be one of my ongoing treatments, Herceptin or Arimidex? Stress? Psoriasis in my ears? The doctors and the nurses had no explanation, remedy, or even hypothesis for it. I was going to have to figure it out for myself.

With each new apprehension of noise in my house, I was driven to find and identify it. One night, I wrote, *I've been lying in bed, night after night, or skulking around, trying to determine its source. That led me to put my ear against my bedroom wall. Yup, the noise is in the wall.* I not only heard the transformer across the road, but also the electricity running through my walls.

Was it time to move again? Summing up my situation, I wrote, *I've made a beautiful house. Cancer broke me apart. The new me is forming, perhaps fueled by my "second menopause," and I'm moving on. Now, I am desperate for quiet.* I thought I'd found peace on a beautiful island, and here I was tormented and exhausted.

I went to a realtor's open house in Langley to find out if it was more peaceful than my cottage. If it was, I was prepared to move, drastic as it seemed. The realtor stayed in the kitchen, somehow keeping a straight face, as I went from room to room, pressing my ear against walls to gauge the level of electrical buzz. The house for sale was no quieter than mine.

I purchased earplugs and a white-noise machine, to no avail. Even with those, I couldn't sleep for longer than an hour or two. With a naval base on the island, perhaps submarines, jets, or other military equipment produced some of the rumbles in the night. Or was it the engine noise of cargo ships passing through the shipping lanes of Puget Sound? When I woke up in the wee hours, trying to identify the noises around me, I wondered if there was a quieter place somewhere. I got up and drove around in the dark, resting in my car if I found a suitable silence. Tranquility never lasted long and soon I was sensing the tones of Mother Earth herself, which some people call the Hum, a persistent, low-frequency droning heard in various parts of the world. When Donald and I were in New Mexico, we heard about the Taos Hum, and I'd been curious what it sounded like. Now that I noticed a Whidbey Hum, I didn't like it. Was the world getting noisier, or was I losing my mind?

When I told Emily I'd been driving around in the dark seeking a quiet place to rest, she may have concluded the latter and worried about me. She mentioned it to Donald. I realized it was difficult for my husband to have such a restless wife, wanting to move again. With Donald's hearing compromised due to tinnitus, he was on the other end of the auditory spectrum and wasn't sympathetic.

When he called, he blamed me for my problem, shouting, "You're making this up. It's all in your head!"

I held the phone away and winced at his fury. Expressing concern is a sign of care. I expected worry, not judgment. But after all the support my family members had given me during the previous months of cancer treatments, it seemed they'd run out of patience and were criticizing me, talking behind my back.

When Stephanie called, she was walking on a Manhattan sidewalk, near the Times Square attraction where she worked. Like her father, she was not interested in my feelings, my fatigue, or the details of my complaints, like which walls in my bedroom were the noisiest. Stephanie scolded me, "You called Emily at 7:30 in the morning with your problems? That's too much to put on her. What are you doing driving around in the middle of the night?"

"Steph, I'm so aggravated by noise, I'm not able to sleep. My brain is getting fuzzier and fuzzier these past few weeks. I don't know why my hearing is so sensitive, but it is. I need to find a quiet place."

I strained to hear my daughter's response over the blare of New York traffic. "There's always noise, Mom. You just have to get used to it."

After the call, I sat in my bedroom, noticing the droning sounds and vibrations in my house. *They want me to suck it up and tough it out, as if I'm the problem? Are my loved ones gaslighting me?* It seemed like they were invalidating my feelings and experiences, making me "wrong" for what I felt, sensed, and needed. Admittedly, it was strange to be so sensitive to noise, but I didn't think I was crazy.

When I asked about hyper-hearing in an online cancer group, I heard from two other women who had similar side effects from their aromatase inhibitor (AI) estrogen blockers. They couldn't sleep well, either. The AIs were looking more and more like the cause of my sleep issues. As an experiment, I stopped taking the AI pills in October, two months after I'd started, and, within days, I was sleeping better and regaining my sonic sanity. One night I went to bed, letting my head sink into the feathery softness of my pillow, and slept till morning.

My sensitivity was a side effect and not "all in my head" as my husband had claimed. I suppose telling me to snap out of it was his way of showing concern. We all moved on, as if giving up an anti-cancer medication was no big deal. Though my family never acknowledged the legitimacy of my complaints, I took comfort in knowing I'd been proactive about investigating and solving my hearing sensitivity problem.

Sometimes we're not just our best advocate, we're our only advocate. Others, including doctors, won't always understand what we're going through. Toni Bernhard wrote in her book, *How to Be Sick: A Buddhist-Inspired Guide for the Chronically Ill and Their Caregivers*, that when care is lacking, "evoking compassion for yourself over what happened is an intelligent response. You're letting yourself know that you understand how disappointing and hard this has been." It can lead to taking action to get better care. Bernhard quotes Maya Angelou: "You may not control all the events that happen to you, but you can decide not to be reduced by them."

The challenges of disease and its treatments come with opportunities for learning, not that such benefits make it any easier in the moment. French writer Hervé Guibert wrote of AIDS, "It was an illness in stages, a very long flight of steps that led assuredly to death, but whose every step represented a unique apprenticeship."

As part of my cancer "apprenticeship," I joined a circle where we read and discussed books about dying by spiritual teachers Stephen Levine and Ram Dass. Contemplating death in good company made it seem less daunting, less lonely. As Ram Dass stated, we're all walking each other home.

Over the course of several months, my hearing gradually desensitized, though I remained more aware of subtle sounds than I used to be. I never again took the Arimidex medication. There were alternative prescriptions for blocking estrogen, but, after what I'd been through, I didn't feel ready to take any of them yet. First, I wanted to find a bigger house.

I still considered noise factors when looking at real estate. If Donald and I were to live together full time, which was not certain, we would need acoustic separation. Donald played music in his studio for hours a day, so, no matter how accomplished and melodic his strumming, I would need a place of quiet for myself and my work. I borrowed a CD of instrumental Irish music from a friend as a stand-in for my husband's guitar playing, bringing the CD and a boombox when I visited homes for sale. When I found a room that was a potential studio for Donald, I played the CD in that room and shut the door. Then I'd walk to the other end of the house. If I could hear the strain of fiddles, the thrum of guitar, or the boom of a bodhran from the primary bedroom or from a room I wanted to use as a home office, that was not the house for me.

One day I drove along the road above Double Bluff Beach in search of an open house there. A long driveway through a meadow led me to a cedar-clad house with endless windows on the water-view side. A man walking between the driveway and an orchard waved to me.

"I'm here for the open house," I said.

The man looked puzzled. "Well, the place is for sale. My wife and I are selling it, but there's no open house today."

I apologized for my mistake and, in friendly island style, we talked for a while anyway. He was a sculptor and used a spacious, separate building as his studio, which was part of the property. He told me the house was built in 1983, which happened to be the year Donald and I got married.

"Come back with your realtor, if you want," the man said, as I turned my car around to depart.

Returning a few days later with a realtor, I saw the place had two levels, both long and thin, as houses go, with plenty of distance from one end to the other. Could this be our parallel play house? When I'd told Donald the property had a separate studio, he'd said he preferred having his music studio in the house. (He'd rather use the sculptor's studio for storage if we bought the place.) A room at the far end of the lower level of the house looked suitable for a music studio, so I started the CD player there. Closing the door, I went upstairs to the bedroom and listened. With that door closed too, I couldn't hear the music. The study next to the bedroom was also quiet. It had sliding doors leading to the deck, perfect for taking breaks from the word processor. The sculptor and his wife used the room as a home office, which would work for me as well. I videotaped the house as I walked through it and sent the video to my husband.

When Donald and I discussed selling the Langley house and buying a new one, we both assumed it would mean less land to take care of, maybe even a condo with no outdoor upkeep. Yet we were both drawn to the parallel house on five acres with its big meadow and little orchard. Daisies dotted the field, reminding me of my long-ago Minnesota meadow—but with views of mountains! The sellers said they never had to cut their tall grass because it was mowed once a year by a farmer who gathered the hay for his cows. My husband, who is a diligent mower, was reassured by that arrangement. He would only have to cut the lawn around the house and orchard.

I told Donald I was in search of a house for both of us. Perhaps he could appreciate what that meant; there could be room for him on the island and in my life.

Studying the listing online and liking what he saw on the video I sent, he suggested, "Put an offer on the house."

I took that as a sign of his trust in me, to make such a big decision from afar. Keeping the Illinois property and selling the Wisconsin cabin, we bought the house on five acres. A retired couple bought the Langley cottage and I moved to the west side of the island.

19

SCANNED AGAIN

*Happiness in life is not determined by marriage. The secret to
happiness lies in building a strong inner self, a self that no
trial or hardship can diminish.*

—DAISAKU IKEDA

I slept well in the new place, though I missed having my
husband there as I adjusted to the spaciousness of a bigger home. It felt a little too big for me alone. Just as no person is
perfect, no particular place is, either. As I'd learned from my astro-
cartography report, every location has a mix of pros and cons.
Yet, the new house felt right to me for this time in our lives. I'd
been happy by myself in my little cottage, and now I was happy
in a home with more room for others to join me. As for pronouns, the parallel house was ours, belonging to both me and my
husband, though he had yet to see it.

As long as Donald had Cassie for company, he was content
to stay at home with her in Illinois. She defined the rhythm of
his days. When she died in June 2018, Donald brought her
wooden box of ashes with him to our new house. I'd already provided bookshelves for his studio, so he placed our dog's remains
on the shelf closest to his desk, keeping her nearby.

When we had daughters living on both coasts, Donald faithfully maintained the middle ground, a meeting place for holidays. Now our children and their partners would all be on Whidbey. My husband was slowly becoming untethered from Illinois, tilting toward the West.

Back on Whidbey, we had a fresh start. When Donald arrived, he was enthusiastic about the new house and all its storage space. He set to work organizing the lower-level room that would serve as his music studio and home office, starting with his new laptop computer.

I remembered when we were first married, after our brief honeymoon to the East Coast, my hubby was completely engrossed in mastering the complex new tools at his investment firm—computers. At home, he studied software and Pascal programming language late into the night. Such a smart cookie! I couldn't help but be impressed by my husband's capabilities and dedication. As a new wife, though, I was already lonely. I justified his behavior, telling myself it was important to him and made him more of an asset to his firm. Donald emerged from his cocoon of computer technology after a few weeks. Throughout our marriage, I was "widowed" on a sporadic basis as my husband immersed himself in pursuing his interests, from bicycle repair to fly fishing, and eventually Irish music.

More than once, I told my husband, "I'm not your twin brother, and I'm not your roommate. I'm your wife. I feel like you've installed me in the house like a piece of furniture. I'd like more chances to enjoy life together and to talk with you." After almost a decade of marriage, when he'd ignored my verbal entreaties, I wrote Donald a succinct but heartfelt letter with the same message, which he read as he sat on our porch. After a few minutes, I walked out to the porch and sat by Donald to see what he had to say. He folded up the letter with no comment and went back inside the house.

All I'd learned from previous relationships or from reading the work of experts, like marital researchers John and Julie Gottman, did no good. Donald was not like anyone I'd ever known (even his identical twin). The standard advice for couples did not apply—or seem to make any difference to him. Yet, I sometimes saw glimmers of brilliance and deep connection that kept me in the marriage, such as when we discussed philosophy or practiced Buddhism together, chanting the Lotus Sutra in harmony. On peaceful days with him, I believed we had good reasons to stay together. On more difficult days, I remained curious—how would the Barbara-Donald story play out?

My husband and I never had an explicit conversation about living together full-time. As usual, Donald was a man of action more than words, speaking only vaguely about someday selling our Midwest house. But his actions led me to believe he was interested in making Whidbey his primary home. Purchasing and furnishing a new house together seemed to indicate the story of Barbara and Donald was not over.

This time, in our Whidbey house, my husband didn't disappear as completely as before. Donald remained gregarious and accessible as he set up his computer and entered his copious music files. We even talked together about our respective computer issues.

Then he said, "I'll make supper. How about salmon and rainbow chard?"

I was included in his equations. What kept our marriage alive? For one thing, our relationship continued to evolve, slipping in and out of the four marital stages described by author John Bradshaw, from codependence (in love with each other) to counter-dependence (power struggle) to independence (individuation and self-actualization) to some measure of cocreation and interdependence (such as setting up our new home together, with space for each of our creative endeavors). More than most couples, Donald and I seemed to benefit from occasional distance from each other.

Therapist Harriet Lerner wrote that "there is no 'right' amount of intimacy for all couples or all relationships." Lerner stressed the need to lower our reactivity and increase our emotional separation as we define ourselves in a relationship, noting, "It is a separateness that ultimately allows for a more solid connectedness with others." If I hadn't had the luxury of solitude in my Langley cottage, I don't think I'd still be married, still willing to be in partnership with someone so different from me.

For another thing, we both continued to challenge our respective blind spots and habits. For instance, sticking up for myself and my home (like when the random man climbed up the ladder by my window) indicated I was becoming more authentic and assertive, changing my karma. Our daily spiritual practice involved a type of human revolution (inner, personal transformation rather than outer, violent revolution) that enhanced self-awareness and our better natures.

As Charlene Spretnak wrote in *States of Grace: The Recovery of Meaning in the Postmodern Age*, applying methods such as meditation changes us. "Our nature, freed from the torturous reactive modes that we ourselves create, reveals itself to be joyous, loving, and filled with gratitude, the roots of celebration." Every morning and evening, as my husband and I faced the mandala of the Gohonzon to recite the Lotus Sutra, we also faced ourselves, for better or worse, and tried to do better. This, in turn, allowed for relationship revolution, appreciating one another and praying for each other's deep-seated happiness, which, again, led to more opportunities for inner transformation, more opening of the lotus blossom to the light.

It also helped that my husband was losing his hearing, so I could mutter under my breath, as needed! Some things should be said and heard, while some things just need to be expressed and released. It's best to have an outlet rather than carry the burden of anger around all day. Sometimes I talked with my friends about my issues or took long walks on my own. I've learned ways to speak up and ways to let things go. A big part of wisdom is living long enough to know better. As Maya Angelou pointed out, when you know better, you do better.

Donald was on Whidbey for much of the winter. For Christmas, we filled our new house with thirty people, including seven of our son-in-law's siblings and their families, most of them from Texas. We set up rows of rectangular tables, like in my old school cafeteria but more festive, and accommodated everybody in our dining room for dinner.

Looking for a way to incorporate a circle, I asked John's mother if she'd help me facilitate a group sharing, and she liked the idea. We gathered in the living room, and I pulled out a talking stick to pass around, getting eyerolls from my daughters. But that was okay; they mostly tolerated my woo-woo ways. In the past, Stephanie and Emily had joined me in talking circles, such as with the Earth Wisdom Community back in the Midwest, so they knew what was coming. *Mom is doing her thing.*

Some people passed the stick on without a word, as if we were playing hot potato, while others seized the stick with relish, sharing a comment, quote, or song. I read a prayer about Saint Bridget kindling the hearth, learning later Bridget was special to John's sister Carol, and John's mother shared a lovely e. e. cummings poem that happened to be a favorite of my dad's. In such moments, I felt we had the magic and serendipity of the circle on our side.

For his turn, Donald brought out his guitar but never played it. Instead, he made a clever musical reference involving tempo and meter that John and his many musical family members appreciated. Then he told a complicated story, ending with a pun that earned him both eyerolls and groans from his listeners.

Late on Christmas Eve, I felt a lump on my chest. I was lying in bed and happened to rub my right collarbone. One of my oncologists told me to feel for something like a frozen pea under the skin when I checked for cancer, and that's what the lump felt like. Donald was half asleep, but I roused him long enough to feel the "pea" for himself.

"Oh," he said, "you should have that checked out." I agreed, but I wouldn't have a chance to be examined until after the holidays.

Before falling asleep, I rehashed the past and fretted over my future. Was the cancer back? Should I have followed my doctors' advice and had a sentinel node biopsy along with my mastectomy—and continued the Arimidex estrogen blocker, though it was driving me mad? Had I waited too long since quitting Arimidex? My doctors had wanted me on the Tamoxifen estrogen blocker, so I started taking it the next day. I had a contradictory wish list for doctors. I wanted them to listen to me and trust my decisions. *And* I wanted them to be informative and persuasive in talking me out of some of those decisions. If I'd been more aware of the ferocity of breast cancer, I would have made different choices.

☙

January 5, I had a scan of my chest and, later, a biopsy. I was afraid the spread of cancer meant stage four, terminal disease. While waiting several days for my results, I could hardly eat or sleep, often lying awake into the wee hours, wondering how I might prepare for my death, if it was imminent. I listed in my mind things I would tell our girls and my special things I'd want them to have.

One day, Emily walked with me at Possession Point on the southern tip of Whidbey Island. As we watched a ferry cross the Salish Sea toward Everett, I told my daughter I was worried about the statistics I'd read. "About thirty percent of people like me who have early-stage breast cancer will have cancer again," I said. "When it returns, it's likely to be incurable, metastatic cancer." Taking in these sobering facts, we walked quietly over the rocky shore for a while. Then Emily showed me a pigeon guillemot burrow and a bald eagle at the top of a Douglas fir. The high-pitched call of the eagle woke me from my worries and brought me back to my senses. As I stood on a trunk of driftwood, I elevated my mind to the eagle in the tree, setting aside my health concerns for the moment. *I am here now with my daughter, feeling well, calmed by the rhythm of the surf, walking with love, and seeing beauty all around me.*

After a few days, I called Dr. Lee, the medical oncologist I thought was "my" doctor in charge of my cancer care. I'd been seeing him for check-ups because he was more experienced than Dr. Chisolm. When Dr. Lee returned my call, I sat down with pencil and paper to take notes. The doctor said the bump by my clavicle was benign, but there was an enlarged lymph node under my right arm that was indeed cancerous.

His words were like static in my brain and terror took my breath away. As my eyes blurred with tears I asked, "Does that mean it's stage four?"

"Though it's a metastatic lymph node, we consider it a regional recurrence of breast cancer. If the cancer hasn't spread beyond the lymph nodes, it's most likely stage two or three."

I took a deep breath, exhaling a sigh of relief. Maybe my new diagnosis wasn't a death sentence, after all. "Oh, that's better news than I expected," I said. "Now, what do I do next?"

"Well, I only handle your medications, so I can't answer that," he said.

I paused. That was news to me. "Who can?"

Dr. Lee had no answer. I felt myself slipping under water, with no one to rescue me. How was I to get the cancer out of my body again and prevent it from spreading? "Oh," I said, choking back my tears, "I wish I had someone overseeing my care! Someone to captain the ship."

"I do too," the doctor said. I've never felt so abandoned as in that moment. I jotted down the oncologist's exact words in disbelief. I was dumbfounded. What use was a health maintenance organization without coordination of care? For this, I'd given up my chance to be treated at the top-notch Seattle Cancer Care Alliance? As disease spread in my body, I had no guidance as to how to proceed to remove it and keep myself alive. I wondered if faulty decisions since my first diagnosis had sealed my fate.

Was I incompetent at navigating the HMO system or were these doctors as cavalier and clueless as they seemed? I knew one thing for sure: They were locked in a system that was less than humane—for them and for their patients. And that system, in turn, was embedded in the profit-driven systems of American health care and health insurance. Amid my own disappointment, my heart ached for those tens of thousands of underinsured Americans who would die each year, unable to pay for the care they needed. Though frustrated with my HMO, I still assumed that, with persistence, I'd find help—and that I'd be able to afford it. My assumptions would be tested as the recurrence of cancer required new rounds of decision-making, considering what to have done and where.

20

....

2B or Not to Be

You have to sniff out joy, keep your nose to the joy trail.
—BUFFY SAINTE-MARIE

$\mathcal{I}$'d never given much thought to my lymphatic system before I had cancer. After the recurrence was identified in the enlarged node under my arm, I'd lie in bed and knead the flesh under my arm until my fingers detected something like a small quail egg, only squishy: the metastatic lymph node. It scared the hell out of me. All but abandoned by my oncologist, I found a surgeon at my HMO, Dr. Clark, to advise me. (My first choice was Dr. Starr who'd done my mastectomy, but she was booked several months out. I didn't want to wait that long.) He said I'd probably need radiation therapy, but first he'd have to scoop out my right axillary (armpit) lymph nodes and check them all for cancer, a procedure I'd avoided during my mastectomy.

Disturbing nodes and vessels has consequences. The lymph system runs through our bodies, bathing every cell and preventing infection. One risk of removing nodes, the filters of the system, is lymphedema (retention of lymphatic fluid), an unpleasant and sometimes debilitating swelling of the arm or other parts of the body. Other risks of axillary surgery include seromas, which are swollen areas where fluids collect, and a painful condition called cording, a taut protrusion running like a ligament down the arm. I worried about disrupting my lymphatic system, but I made the appointment for an axillary lymph node dissection (ALND) with Dr. Clark. My enlarged node and, most likely, its neighbors were now conduits for cancer, rather than a helpful part of my immune system. They had to come out.

Warned that some people are permanently affected by lymphedema, I thought about what necessitated the strenuous use of people's arms. Were there activities I should enjoy *before* surgery in case my right arm was damaged and I was unable to engage in them afterward? One came to mind: *Ziplining.* I'd never been on a zipline, and I really wanted to go flying through the treetops!

I approached my husband to gauge his interest, using our upcoming thirty-sixth anniversary as an excuse. "Hey, Donald, I found a farm and forest on Camano Island that has ziplines. Want to go ziplining for our anniversary? It's easy to get there," I added, "because Camano is right next to Whidbey and has a bridge from the mainland." I gave Donald a big smile to show how much fun I expected it to be. In return, he gave me a long-suffering look, as though he was too old for such high-speed, aerial adventures. "Well," I admitted, "we'd have to go a couple weeks before our anniversary because my surgery is March 11. It's got to be before that, while I still have use of all my limbs." To humor me, Donald agreed to my air-brained scheme and I made reservations.

The weather was cold and snowy when we arrived at the zipline, so we were surprised to see a half dozen other customers waiting to enter the canopy of the forest. Our two guides gave us an orientation and set us up with our harnesses and helmets. Then each of us climbed to a high platform, got hooked up to strong wires, launched ourselves into space (some of us with a loony laugh or a shriek), and glided from one tall Douglas fir to another. Both Donald and I had big smiles on our faces as we whooshed along through the chilly air.

The harness supported me without requiring much use of my arms, but I liked holding onto the straps for stability. Trusting the wires, my harness, and my own functioning body, I adored having freedom to soar. Midway in our series of ziplines, we came to a clearing in the forest and were surprised to see a campfire waiting there for us. We touched down on earth, sipped hot tea, and warmed ourselves by the fire before completing the course. With all my senses activated, I thought, *Yes, this is life! I want to live while I'm alive.* Doing something purely for fun helped me face the treatment that lay ahead.

The next day, I looked through my pre-op instructions and noticed the power of attorney form where I could state my end-of-life preferences. I hadn't bothered to fill one out before. I considered that if I was going to die, I'd want to be with my loved ones, preferably at home or in hospice, and not be poked and prodded by doctors all day long. I filled out the form, thinking, *I want to die in peace—and not too soon.*

On the day of my ALND, Dr. Clark was running late. A nurse said the doctor was completing a procedure that turned out to be more difficult than expected. I waited on a gurney for three hours with an IV in my arm, with Donald nearby. A compressor circulated warm air through an inflatable blanket to maintain my body temperature. Its noise made conversation difficult, but my husband wasn't much of a converser in hospitals, anyway. I meant to use the time to visualize a safe, smooth surgery, but my mind skittered away, unable to focus on any-thing specific. Instead, I closed my eyes and tried to rest amid the bustle going on outside my cubicle.

When the surgeon showed up, looking frazzled and rushed, I was taken into the operating room, after which I don't remember anything, till I awoke in great pain in an overly bright recovery area. The number of axillary lymph nodes to be removed for the spread of breast cancer varies widely, from about ten to about forty. Donald told me Dr. Clark took out twelve.

As an attendant wheeled me out to get ready to go home, Donald and I saw our daughter waiting for us, which made me feel better. "Emily," I said, "you came to see me!" As my Percocet medication kicked in, I saw swirling colors around her face, which I liked almost as much as the pain relief.

☙

One week later, Dr. Clark called with a pathology report. "Three of the twelve nodes showed cancer," he said. "We consider that stage 2B." I thanked him for calling and for doing the surgery. Then I hung up the phone and did a happy dance around the kitchen island, waving my good left arm and shouting, "Woo-hoo!" My cancer was considered regional—and not terminal, as I had feared.

Still, I had to contend with the aftermath of the surgery. I regretted not finding a way to have the wonder woman, Dr. Starr, as my surgeon again. I also kicked myself for agreeing to a surgery date during Mercury retrograde, a phase known to as-trologists as a time of mishaps, glitches, and setbacks. Dr. Clark did what had to be done to remove the nodes, and he'd kept our agreement for the use of a laryngeal mask, which I appreciated.

But, as was common with ALND, nerves and tissues were damaged, leaving me with pain and dysfunction. I was on more painkillers than I had needed with previous surgeries. In Dr. Susan Love's book, I read that chronic pain is common after axillary dissection, so it was hard to predict how long mine would last.

Complications required five trips to the doctor to drain my bloated seroma and eight trips to receive physical therapy. I had nerve pain, and my range of arm motion was limited. My right arm puffed up enough with lymphedema for the physical therapist to order me a compression sleeve to minimize the swelling. As with my doctor's tip to shop for a prosthesis at Nordstrom, my physical therapist gave me an insider tip to get my stretchy sleeve at a specialty shoe store in Everett. (I would not have guessed to look there.) I'd pull on the tight tube before lifting bags of groceries, kayaking, or anything likely to provoke more pain and swelling.

When my cratered armpit healed, I went to Moon, a lymph massage therapist on the island. The opposite of deep tissue massage, her touch was so gentle, I was transported to a magical place, as if effervescent fairies wearing ballet slippers made of flower petals were dancing over my skin. For the hundredth time, I gave thanks for the magic of Whidbey Island and its people.

I bought a new Bundt pan and made a luscious lemon-blueberry pound cake for me and my husband. Not only did Donald give me flowers on our anniversary, but my sisters and brother sent me a bouquet. What a sweet surprise!

Their card read, "Dearest Dilly, these flowers come from all your sibs, to cheer your day and tickle your ribs."

My ribs would be sore for some time to come, but, as I prepared for a summer of radiation therapy, I was feeling better day by day.

21

BEAM ON

Suddenly, it became clear to me that a battle against illness is a battle for total and correct information.
—TINA TURNER

$\mathcal{I}$n the spring of 2019, I had a weighty decision to make about charged subatomic particles known as protons. After physicists figured out, ninety years ago, how to produce those particles, protons were found to be useful in treating cancer. Following surgery to remove cancerous lymph nodes under my right arm, Dr. Lee prescribed standard radiation treatments to eradicate any cancer left behind. I considered both proton and standard radiation for treating my recurring breast cancer. Which was better in my situation?

As difficult as having cancer was, I found the decision-making process about treatment options for the disease just as difficult. There's a certain torture in having to make life and death decisions in the face of limited and often biased information, along with the prospects of major risks and side effects to consider. Each choice can have huge consequences. I wished for someone I trusted to advise me, yet it seemed my doctors often had the same script.

"No, we don't have cold caps to help you retain your hair during chemo, and we won't even try to get them."

Or they'd say, "This is the standard of care."

What if I wasn't the standard patient? Their advice seemed aimed more at moving me swiftly through their system than answering my questions.

The standard radiation treatment for breast cancer is not proton therapy but photon therapy, similar to X-rays. The purpose of standard photon radiation is to kill unseen cancer in a process a nurse described to me as "mopping up any stray cancer cells." It was a follow-up treatment after having my cancerous lymph nodes removed. I would have dots tattooed on my chest to mark the boundaries of treatment so radiation could be beamed within that broad boundary. (Each area of the body can be safely radiated only once, so they left the permanent dots for future reference. The area within those dots must be avoided if I ever receive radiation again.)

Like everything they offered, my HMO doctors said this was "the standard" for my situation. When I asked about the newer proton therapy, the doctors on my oncology team said they didn't have that option at their facilities and that its efficacy for breast cancer was unproven.

I found the doctors' quick dismissal frustrating. Proton radiation is more focused and precise than other kinds of radiation. Unlike standard radiation, which keeps traveling all the way through one's body, protons are beamed to a target and stop there. That's important when trying to avoid zapping healthy organs while killing the cancer. My treatment would be on my right side, away from my heart. Still, my lung, bones, and other areas of my body could be damaged by the beams of standard radiation.

To learn more about my options, I made an appointment for

a consultation at a proton center. A doctor sat with me in a consultation room and briefly informed me about the value of proton radiation therapy. When he understood my insurance would not cover what he offered, he switched gears. I was taken aback as he started talking like a used-car salesman.

"If you pay out-of-pocket, we can offer you treatments for a reduced price," he said, naming a figure far below the going rate, which I knew would be at least ten times as much.

I felt more like a customer than a patient and tried to back up to the information-gathering part of the consultation. "How does the pencil-thin proton beam work with breast cancer? Does it mop up stray cancer cells in the wide area of my chest the way standard radiation does?"

The proton radiation doctor didn't even try to answer. He was too busy pulling out his calendar. "When shall we have your first appointment? When can you come in?"

"I have to think about it," I said, as I picked up my purse to depart. Yes, I might be willing to pay the price of a used car if it meant saving my life or even an organ, but I wasn't convinced it would.

When Donald and I lived in the Chicago area, we liked to visit Fermi National Accelerator Laboratory with our children, and I understood some of what was required to generate protons. With the help of a magnet, particles are slung around at tremendous speeds in the underground loop of the cyclotron, like some kind of sci-fi carnival ride. At Fermilab, their magnet weighs six hundred tons. The yearly budget for their physics experiments is hundreds of millions of dollars. No doubt the equipment at the proton center was expensive as well. Perhaps the doctor at the center made me such a tempting offer because he needed more patients in order to pay the bills.

I knew proton technology was helping many people, especially those with brain tumors, but I didn't know whether it would be effective in eliminating breast cancer. I went to bed asking for a sign, whether it came from science, angels, or my own intuition. I needed help deciding between the two types of radiation to treat my cancer—something more than the scripts I was hearing from the doctors, each of whom had vested interest in my choices.

As the morning sun brightened our bedroom, I awoke with the word Michael on my lips, a name sparking two images: Archangel Michael and our nephew Michael.

I was not raised with knowledge of angels, but I became fond of the angel Michael as he came to my attention over the years. For instance, a psychic named Beverly told me she saw him watching over me. How comforting, especially when I learned Michael, one of the four archangels, is considered a healer and a warrior. In art, he is sometimes depicted slaying a dragon, which was the kind of help I needed as I faced the dragon of cancer— and my own confusion.

I remembered when angels in the cemetery near my cottage in Langley caught my eye. This occurred due to running into the same woman, Kay, several times there. I liked to take walks up the hill from my house and through the woodsy cemetery. I saw Kay sitting by her mother's grave, which awaited a grave marker, and we began talking. She was sad and I listened to her. Kay had consecrated the spot with some beach stones and a knee-high angel. One day she pointed out to me that the angel had been damaged.

"My brother left a candle burning in her lap and now she's ruined," she lamented.

"Oh, no," I said, picking up a leaf from the ground. "Let's see if we can clean her up." I used the leaf to rub off some soot from the angel's skirt and showed it to Kay. "See, it comes off." Slumped in her plastic lawn chair, Kay ignored my chirpy optimism, showing no motivation to scrub the ornamental angel. So, I went back to the gravesite the next day when she wasn't there. I brought a bucket with soap, water, and a rag and went to work on the holy lady. I wanted to surprise Kay by cleaning up the figure that was special to her.

As I worked, I noticed the winged lady had something in common with me. We were both missing a breast. My right breast had been surgically removed, and the angel's left breast was partially melted away by the candle flame. Well, her scar was more like a lumpectomy than a mastectomy. I don't know if she was made of resin or plastic or something else, but she had been burned and damaged. I felt a sense of sisterhood with her and gave extra attention to cleaning the soot and candle drippings off the angel's pale chest. Then I placed her back on the grave.

With a wet rag in my hand, I looked around for something else to clean and my eyes landed on a dark, handsome angel on a pedestal. Twice the height of the pale angel, this one looked like cast stone that had turned green and black with age. I walked over to the sculpture and cleaned him too. The color remained the same, but leaves, pine needles, and cobwebs were brushed away. "Looking good!" I said, not that he cared about appearances. For all I knew, he could have been a standard-issue, archless angel, but it seemed to me he was Archangel Michael. Afterward, whenever I took walks through the cemetery, I spent a moment of contemplation with him.

Different faiths and cultures have different designated helpers. I didn't mind exploring beyond the *shoten zenjin* (protective forces) of Buddhism. Maybe they were just different names and faces for the same archetypal powers, whether those powers reside in myself, nature, or another world. I had asked for help getting the best treatment and the name of that angel came to me. Perhaps, as Beverly said, a winged one was watching over me.

Michael is also the name of a family member, and I said it out loud to my husband as we were waking up. "Say, isn't your nephew, Michael, an oncologist? Maybe I could contact him to discuss my radiation dilemma."

"He's busy with his pediatric oncology fellowship," Donald reminded me.

Michael was the only child of Donald's twin brother, David, and his wife, Sherry, who lived in Maryland, and we rarely saw him.

"I doubt if he'll respond, since we've barely been in touch for the past decade or so," I said. "And he was such a quiet, contemplative kid, I never really got to know him. But I'll send him an email and see what happens."

After lunch, I sent a brief message to Michael to say hi and outline my radiation options for treating my recurrence of breast cancer. Did he have any thoughts about it or any research material he could suggest? Then I went to take a nap. Within minutes, our home phone rang and I ignored it. *Junk call*, I thought. But when my cell phone rang, I was curious and answered it.

It was Michael. He had already emailed me back with relevant articles and suggestions and, yes, it was him trying to reach me on our landline. He'd asked his parents for my cell number.

What ensued was an honest and informative conversation. Michael had cancer himself as a young man and expressed empathy for me. I felt right away he had my best interests at heart. He also understood what it was like for me dealing with doctors who had their own agendas.

As a pediatric oncologist, Michael worked with children, so he was not familiar with the use of radiation for breast cancer. He helped me as much as he could and directed me to resources where I could find more information.

"Here's my phone number," he said, "and my pager number in case I'm in a meeting. Call anytime. Family comes first."

I was so moved by his unexpected warmth, accessibility, and sincerity, tears sprang to my eyes.

When people claim there are times to be grateful for cancer, it may be hard to believe. But, believe me, this was one of those times. Because of cancer, I got to know a side of our nephew I never knew before. He's become a man who is humanistic and attentive, generous with both his knowledge and his caring. His patients and students are lucky to have him.

After the phone call with Michael, I read two more research articles and then felt confident to make up my mind. I would stick with the standard radiation, not only because it was cheaper but because I felt it was the better, more effective option for me. Plus, the standard treatments could be done at a hospital in Everett, a nearby location with staff who made me feel at ease.

Over the summer, I had my six weeks of radiation. Every weekday, I awaited my turn for treatment, watching for the "BEAM ON" sign on the wall to go dark and the thick, heavy door to slide open. When the previous patient departed, I was called into the dim little room and lined up on a narrow table in the exact same position every time, lying on my back with arms raised. As the radiation technicians drew blue lines on my chest marking treatment boundaries, we had conversations about the capabilities of the Trilogy machine crouching over my body or, as we got to know each other, a wider range of topics.

One day I walked in wearing my usual flimsy hospital gown

and carrying a striped cotton purse. A technician noticed my bag and said, "You look ready for the beach."

"Yeah," I told him, "I'm going to catch some rays!" I smiled like I was about to relax on the sand, and he laughed at my bit of radiation humor.

When that same young man found out I'm a nature lover, he said, "Check out Mount Si. It's a good hike to the top and there are friendly birds there." I liked that scenario. Left alone in the room, Trilogy clicking and whirring above me, I closed my eyes and imagined birds in the mountains.

In the waiting room, I met a patient named Jenny who already had her bilateral mastectomy and was now receiving radiation therapy. She considered having plastic surgery when she recovered from her radiation treatments, wondering whether to have implants or "flap" surgery that uses fat and skin from the patient's own body to form new breasts. Or should she remain flat? Jenny was fifty years old, twelve years younger than me, and it was a tough decision for her. We sat together in the hospital waiting room almost every day for weeks, conversing until our names were called for treatment. Many of the other patients were men waiting for prostate cancer radiation and some of them were talkative too. But most days Jenny and I sought each other out.

One day she confided, "My husband says he's sure I'll have the surgery because I'll want to be whole."

I leaned back in my chair to assess my reaction, feeling a vinyl chill through the gap in my hospital gown. That statement did not sit well with me. Of course, the question of plastic surgery was deeply personal to Jenny and her husband, yet I wanted to weigh in on the implications of what it means to "be whole." After a minute or two, I said, "The way I see it, you are whole the way you are. Whether you have breasts or not, you are whole." I considered my own feelings about my missing mammary and added, "I am whole the way I am."

The next time I went to the hospital, Jenny avoided me. I looked her way, but she would not meet my gaze. I would have felt rejected, but I could understand if she needed time to sort out her feelings. For a few days we sat separately and chatted with other patients.

I especially liked talking with Arnold, the most miserable-looking person in the room. He sat with his head slumped into his hand, his skinny elbow on the plastic armrest, which seemed a reasonable response to what we were going through. Cumulative radiation can cause fatigue, so I asked him if that was the case.

"Are you near the end of your radiation treatments?" He shook his head slightly to say no. I waited.

Arnold finally raised his head and looked my way. "I'm halfway through. It's the chemotherapy combined with the radiation that gets to me."

Oh, that I understood. Chemo alone had flattened me during my first round of treatments, and I said so. I empathized with Arnold and made a point of greeting him each day. When Arnold finished his radiation treatments for prostate cancer, those of us in the waiting room applauded for him.

Jenny warmed up to me again, and we resumed our daily conversations. She eventually decided against reconstruction and told me she was at peace with her decision. I've since seen a photo of her rocking a ruffled shirt that complements her new body. Jenny is as whole as ever, and would be, regardless of her decision.

After several weeks of treatments, my radiated skin turned

pink but was not severely burned. Discomfort was easily reme-died with calendula lotion. Damage from the radiation passing through my body could show up years from now, but the treat-ments to eradicate cancer went well, as far as the doctors could tell.

I emailed Michael to let him know I was successfully treated and how much I appreciated his support. An English major be-fore he went to med school, Michael likes to write, so we have that in common. He reads some of my writing about cancer, when he gets a minute, and gives me feedback. Now I have no evidence of disease, and I have no evidence of distance from our busy and beloved nephew, Michael.

22

PATH OF THE HEART

*I stop thinking about survival as a scramble up a steep, slippery
slope back to the life I'd known, and start to think about its
root, sur-vivere—living beyond—and of joyfully,
exuberantly, striding straight out of the canyon into the
unknown.*

—DIANA LINDSAY

arlos Castaneda wrote in *The Teachings of Don Juan: A
Yaqui Way of Knowledge* of a question elders ask us about
our life choices. "Does this path have a heart? One path makes
for a joyful journey. The other path will make you curse your
life."

I was realizing that no matter how confused my mind, I
could trust the quiet, often humorous voice inside me. The more
I heeded my heart, the brighter, clearer, and more joyful my
path.

In mid-July, I finished six weeks of radiation therapy for
breast cancer. Three days later, my husband and I caught an early
ferry from Whidbey Island to the mainland and then drove two
hours to Crystal Mountain. We stopped at Alpine Inn and got
our key and room number, which, thankfully, didn't end in thirteen this time.

A woman at the desk told us to keep an eye out for a family of silver foxes in the area, adding, "Remember, they're wildlife —a lot of fun to watch but give them space to do their thing."

We said we would. Following a guidebook I'd brought along, Donald and I explored Mount Rainier National Park, starting at Naches Peak Loop Trail. The white petals of avalanche lilies spread across the field like stars, leading us into a wonderland, joined by purple phlox as we got to higher elevations. The guidebook said the loop was three miles long, rising to an altitude of 5,800 feet. Still recovering from radiation, I wondered if I could make it the whole way and have enough energy to enjoy the rest of our visit. Our walking sticks came in handy, crunching our way along the rocky trail. With a new view or lake around every bend, we were both motivated to keep going. As we rounded Naches Peak, the bright snowy face of Mount Rainier appeared.

"Look, Donald, the mountain is out!" I said, using the local phrase for Takhoma's appearance.

"The mountain is out," he echoed with a smile, amused at our newbie attempts to sound like experienced Pacific Northwesterners.

In the evening, before having supper at Alpine Inn, Donald and I walked up the hill to the grounds of Crystal Mountain ski resort, quiet in the off-season. Ahead of us, by the far side of the road, I saw a flash of charcoal-gray fur followed by a luxuriously fluffy tail tipped in white. Pointing, I whispered to Donald, "What is that?" Just then the animal sat down in the road and two smaller versions emerged from a hole in the ground to join her. "Oh," I sighed, "it's the silver fox mother and her kits! So beautiful."

Donald nodded, pausing to watch them. As I moved around our side of the road, snapping photos, my husband stood still and gave them space. Goofy packages of joy, the young foxes played and toppled over each other until their mother led them back to their den. Nature was once again conspiring to make me happy.

We continued walking and came to a bell tower, about twenty feet tall, next to a parking lot of an administrative building. I stopped and took Donald's arm. "A bell! I wonder if they use it as an alarm, like for weather alerts or ski accidents." I turned to Donald. "You know what I'm thinking?" I said, assuming it was obvious.

"No idea."

Already starting to walk toward the building, I reminded him, "I never got to ring a bell when I finished chemotherapy, and now I'm done with radiation. Maybe they'll let me ring this one!"

My husband stopped in his tracks, wanting no part of my brainstorm. Attracting attention to himself rarely appealed to him. When I entered the chalet-style building, I spoke to a man at his desk. I was prepared to tell him my reason for wanting to ring the bell, thinking he would require persuasion, but he didn't ask. "I saw the bell tower out there and I was wondering if I may ring the bell."

Hardly glancing up, the fellow said, "Yeah, okay," and returned to his work.

I found myself disappointed not to have a chance to tell my end-of-treatments story. I went back outside to the bell and invited Donald to join me. Instead, as with the foxes, he stood apart and gave me space to do my thing.

For a moment, it seemed a little pathetic to carry out the bell-ringing ritual in the vast silence of a deserted ski resort with no one to cheer me on, but what the hell. I thought about both my alarming diagnoses of cancer. Now, instead of sounding an alarm, I was signaling relief. I tugged on the thick rope over and over till the clapper hit the metal side with a resounding clang. *This is it,* I thought. *Ring out!* The tones of the big gleaming bell bounced off Crystal Mountain and reverberated down the valley.

My husband may have been a little embarrassed by my jubilation, but he was there, nearby, just as he'd kept me company as we rounded every bend in the trail. Donald was a steady support to me and our family. Our relationship dynamics might not work for everybody, but with extra effort on both our parts, they worked for us. The space between us had its advantages, giving me freedom to hear myself, make my own decisions, and ring my bell. We went and had a delicious dinner of salmon and Bavarian pho at the inn and then had a deep sleep, side-by-side, as one.

Our love story was not the same or as romantic as my parents' love story; mine was more dispersed, interwoven with many colorful strands. Our marriage was a long, vibrant strand, but not the only one in the loom of my life.

Spiritual teacher Gary Zukav wrote in *Soul Stories*, "The cells in your body love each other. Your blood loves your heart and lungs. Your spine loves your brain. Your body is a love story that continues day after day."

An awakened heart is the song of life. In his book, *Consolations: The Solace, Nourishment and Underlying Meaning of Everyday Words*, poet David Whyte wrote, "Solace is found in allowing the body's innate wisdom to come to the fore, the part of us that already knows it is mortal," adding that solace accompanies us through the mixture of pain and beauty in the world.

I take solace in my humanity, caress the warm silk of my skin, and hold my own hand. I'm living love stories of myself, my body, my marriage, my family, my friends, hummingbirds, trees, the earth, the sea—all interconnected.

Ever since I was diagnosed with cancer, people sent me affection and support, and geographical distance was no obstacle. I received it. My gratitude flowed back to them just as swiftly. For instance, I wrote a letter to my mentor, Ikeda Sensei, when I was diagnosed with a recurrence of cancer. As he was in his nineties and living in Japan, I did not expect a response. Then one day during radiation, I sensed his presence, as if he was in my hospital treatment room chanting with me. I felt elated, wanting to jump up to greet him, but remembered I was required to lie completely still on the radiation table. Instead, I wept with gratitude, tears dripping down the side of my face and trickling into my ear. *Could it be he read my letter and was praying for me?* The next day I received a phone call from one of Sensei's assistants who said my mentor received my message and sent me his prayers. *I know*, I thought with amazement, as I offered my thanks to the caller.

We are all connected, holding each other in one way or another.

23

CANCER HAS ITS POWER
AND I HAVE MINE

*Everything has its wonders, even darkness and silence, and I
learn whatever state I am in, therein to be content.*
—HELEN KELLER

ecurrence of disease can be hard to predict and difficult
to detect. In the past, doctors periodically checked breast
cancer survivors' blood panels, MRI, and PET/CT scans for
signs of new, spreading, or recurring cancers, but the current
practice for early-stage patients is to wait until there are specific
symptoms before ordering any kind of test beyond a mammogram.

The scans themselves can adversely affect health, and as
surgeon Kristi Funk wrote in her book about breast cancer, "Early
detection of metastatic disease offers no survival advantage
when compared to waiting for symptoms, finding metastases,
and then pursuing treatments." Offering only an annual mammogram of my remaining breast, my HMO put the burden on
me, the patient, to be vigilant about any suspicious symptoms, a
responsibility that made me nervous. How would I know when a
headache, an aching bone, or a cough meant my cancer had

spread to my brain, bones, or lungs (the most typical places for it to spread)? I tried to pay attention to my body without obsessing over the "what ifs."

While manually examining my chest at the end of 2019, I'd found a suspicious bump by my collarbone and had a chest scan showing no problem with the bump but revealing a cancerous lymph node. Now, a year later, after radiation treatment for my cancer recurrence, a refreshingly proactive member of my oncology team wanted me to have another CT scan. Specifically, she wanted to check some nodules in my lung that had showed up on my last scan and to look for other trouble spots.

Donald drove me to my HMO on the mainland. I was grateful to have any kind of follow-up. My hope was to be free and clear of cancer by the end of the year; the scan would let me know if that was the case.

As I waited in a little room at the medical center, I peeked out the door at a life-size Elvis Presley in the corridor. The cardboard cutout wore hospital scrubs that inexplicably had HANGRY written across the fabric. Was the King hungry and angry? I tried to think of one of his song lyrics that would make this relevant and could only come up with "hound dogs" and "blue suede shoes." Elvis was also sporting green beads and a fuzzy red Santa hat, which were at least in keeping with the season. Though it reminded me of all the holiday things I'd rather be doing that day, like wrapping gifts, I appreciated a little hospital humor to ease the tension.

Fear and faith rode together while I waited for tests and their results. Once you've had cancer, any scan can be a cause for anxiety, or as some patients call it, *scanxiety.* (*Chemoflage,* meaning to hide the effects of chemotherapy, is another cancer-inspired neologism.) In my case, it wasn't the tumors I dreaded most, it was the treatments and their damages and side effects. I'd never felt even a twinge from the cancer itself, though there was always the bone-chilling awareness it could kill me at some point.

※

I remembered meeting a horse named Checar ten years ago in Tucson. He was a little wild and could probably kill me in certain circumstances, but I wasn't afraid of him. Part palomino and part quarter horse, he caught my attention when I saw him in the stables near my casita. I signed up for a trail ride in hopes I could get to know him or at least stroke his long white mane. Before heading into the sagebrush, we riders gathered in the barn for instruction. The trail guide, Nina, asked, "On a scale of one to ten, how scared are you of horses?"

"Eleven," proclaimed a young man. I was surprised he would rate his fear that high. With nervous laughter, the other seven or eight people admitted to high numbers as well.

When it came to me, I wanted to say zero. As a toddler, I took a tumble and hit my head when I tried to ride a stick horse up my aunt's basement stairs, but I'd never been hurt by the real thing. Having been around horses at friends' farms and at Bay Lake stables, I realized you had to be careful to avoid being kicked or thrown. Our daughter Emily had recently had an accident when she and her horse went over a jump. They both fell. Emily broke her arm, requiring surgery. My Mom-alarm bells went off and I rushed to take care of her. But was I afraid of horses? No, I had a healthy respect for them. That was different.

I said, "One."

Maybe Nina assigned horses based on those numbers. For

whatever reason, she gave me my dream horse, Checar. I was in rapture as I settled into the saddle and rode into the Sonoran Desert, reminded of poet James Wright's reaction to caressing the ear of a Minnesota mare: "Suddenly I realize/ That if I stepped out of my body I would break/ Into blossom."

Cacti saluted along the trail, and blue sky went on forever above us. Along with the hoofbeats of my horse, I heard the raspy call of a cactus wren flying by and the sweet whistle of a thrasher in the distance. Allowing space between me and the other riders, I softly sang my awe and gratitude, mixing my own simple rhymes—*you and me, riding free*—with Joe Cocker's "You Are So Beautiful," the Unitarian Universalist hymn, "For the Beauty of the Earth," and whatever else came to mind.

Patting the palomino's warm, strong neck, the color of butterscotch, and running my fingers through his frothy mane, I was enchanted. As I rocked in my saddle with the calming rhythm of the horse, I ran out of words, settling into a silent way of knowing, perhaps something like the spirit of poetry described by Joy Harjo. "It is a kind of resurrection light; it is the tall ancestor spirit who has been with me since the beginning, or a bear, or a hummingbird. It is a hundred horses running the land in a soft mist, or it is a woman undressing for her beloved in the firelight."

Taking a deep breath, I held that holiness close to my heart, to save some for later.

When we returned to the stables, I dismounted, and Nina took the reins to lead the horse back to his stall. Checar lingered by my side and resisted her pull. She harumphed that he'd never done that before.

"It's because I sang to him," I said.

❦

Some of the oldest artifacts in the world, before plows—or even agriculture—existed, were musical instruments, including a flute made from a bear femur fifty thousand years ago. Humans have known for a very long time that music has powers of enchantment, healing, and transformation. What could my cancer song be? Not a love song, of course, for a sneaky disease, but, like riding Checar, it would be a hymn to transport me beyond anxiety, beyond fear.

Cancer has its power and I have mine, I thought. Yes, disease could kill me someday, but I didn't want to make my own body —or even cancer—my enemy. I admired those who declared war against cancer and battled with all their might, but that was not in keeping with my temperament.

As he faced his own cancer, author Brian Doyle noted in *A River of Song: Notes on Wonder* that none of the diagnosed people he knew "ever used military or sporting metaphors that I remember. All of them spoke of endurance, survival, the mad insistence of hope, the irrepressibility of grace, the love and affection and laughter and holy hands of their families and friends and churches and clans and tribes."

This was true of my friend Kelly, an extraordinary man in our Whidbey community, who employed his creativity to communicate with his brain tumor, with peace in his heart. Perhaps my song, in honor of that friend—and Checar—could be about life, love, and courage rather than death, defeat, and despair. It could be something as grounding as the old Shaker hymn, "'Tis a Gift to Be Simple" or as uplifting as Beethoven's "Ode to Joy." Perhaps when I most needed it, I would hum that tune and know those words. If I listened with my heart, I'd hear it.

The scan I had almost a year ago showed a "metastatic enlarged lymph node" under my right arm, which was alarming. But this scan didn't have to be. I kept my nerves in check, focusing on my breathing till I was called into the imaging room. Lying on my back, I let the machine slide me through the donut hole of the scanner.

As I left the room, the technician told me the results would show up as a message from my doctor in a week. They came in that very day when Donald and I got home. I read the online message and reported to my husband, "The nodules haven't grown. And there are no signs of cancer. I made my goal—all clear at the end of the year!" We gave each other a big bear hug, then put up our noble fir in the living room and started hanging ornaments.

24

WHAT'S LEFT

When you regain a sense of your life as a journey of discovery,
you return to rhythm with yourself.
—JOHN O'DONOHUE

I figure things out as I go along, not always knowing what
I'm doing. When I don't have the answers, I live with the
questions as I try to decipher clues around me. In the anthology,
Living the Questions, poet Mark Nepo suggested we be open to
messages available to us and "we will be found by our teachers
repeatedly—be they the moon, the thief, or the tiger—until we
can uncover their meaning."

Some of my decisions have worked out well, some not so
well. Unlike those who yearn for power, harmony is my goal.
When relationships are out of whack, so am I. In all my struggles
over the last few years, my biggest decision was to move to
Whidbey Island. I left my husband because I needed some space.
Or should I say my husband stayed in Illinois because *he* needed
some space? Whatever the case, two thousand miles seemed
about right. I didn't know if we'd ever live together again. The
more time I had alone on the island, the more I knew I would be
okay whether I was married or not. As it turned out, our bond
stretched but did not break. If classrooms can make room for

neurodiversity, maybe relationships can too. We evolved, reviving our relationship through quiet times, raucous times, and the love of family. Because I chose a spouse so different from me, our marriage cracked my life open—and the view was worth it.

I miss my old friends back in the Midwest and find ways to keep in touch with them, but I sense this place, the Pacific Northwest, is where I need to be. Now that I've established a home base on the island, I feel free enough and safe enough to know myself better and in turn, get to know other people better, wherever they may be. I've learned we each have a purpose, and we fulfill our missions best by being our true, unique selves. I contribute to the world by being me, not by shapeshifting to meet others' expectations. As an added bonus, being authentic is good for my health.

I liked living in my little Langley cottage, yet I've come to realize I liked designing it just as much. I spent months fussing over details and trying to resolve practical issues, like the odd shape of my primary closet with no accommodation for a rod to hang my clothes, all at a time when I sorely needed distraction from my disintegrating marriage. Instead of fretting at night, I fell asleep mentally arranging furniture and imagining paint colors. How could I put so much into its manifestation, from empty lot to two-story dream home, and then move to another house? I've found the joy in creation is never lost. The sanctuary of the cottage served its purpose, and then I moved on to a different configuration of my life, just as engaging.

Going through cancer and trying to understand how I got sick were my biggest struggles.

I was neither emotionally nor mentally prepared to face the reality of my poison-cut-burn regimen. Playwright Eve Ensler (also called V) is no stranger to trauma, yet she wrote in her book, *In the Body of the World: A Memoir of Cancer and Connection*, about cancer pushing her to her limits. "And it was there, dangling on that edge, that I was forced to let go of everything that didn't matter, to release the past and be burned down to essential matter. It was there I found my second wind." I'm still catching my breath.

Though one of my priorities in facing disease was to gather useful information, I never had a chance to have my genes tested until recently. Thanks to the resources at Seattle Cancer Care Alliance, I took a blood test of more than fifty genes associated with cancer. Because my family history did not suggest hereditary factors, genetic testing was not offered to me earlier and was not covered by insurance. I had to pay for it myself, which I gladly did for the sake of my daughters. Was there anything they might inherit to put them at risk?

When the results came back, both my genetic counselor and I were surprised to learn that I have a CHEK2 mutation signifying increased risk for breast cancer. The CHEK2 gene is supposed to help prevent tumors, but mine isn't working.

More than simply suspecting that gene as a *factor*, the counselor said, "Your cancer was caused by CHEK2."

I will be alerting our daughters and my siblings and cousins to this significant genetic risk factor, though I don't know which parent passed it on to me. Just because I have it doesn't mean family members will have it too, and I hope they don't. I told my genetic counselor my theory about chronic distress making me more susceptible to cancer, and she didn't rule it out. There may be multiple pieces to the puzzle.

My cancer and treatments led me to transform my life. Restoring my health, I regained personal harmony, relying on my body once again. It wasn't all miserable. With such rough incidents to polish my life, how can I help but shine? As Ensler observed after surviving cancer, wishing and worrying cannot save us; only kindness can.

Illness is a dive into what it means to reach out, open our hearts, and be vulnerable, foregoing bravado and other facades as we accept care from others. The more serious the illness, the deeper the dive.

Buddhist sage Nichiren wrote eight centuries ago in a letter now called "New Year's Gosho," "Misfortune comes from one's mouth and ruins one, but fortune comes from one's heart and makes one worthy of respect."

As Donald and I lead more from our hearts, establishing a more spacious marriage, I feel I can laugh again, with room for both of us to be ourselves. As we gather with loved ones or explore the conifer forests (me communing with a tree, forehead on bark, and him waiting without comment on the trail), we create more interlocking memories each day. The weight of our almost four decades of shared history helps ground our marriage.

As unexpected issues arise, we deal with them. For instance, when we bought the parallel play house, we were told there was a guy who would harvest the four-acre meadow every summer so we'd never have to mow it ourselves. Unfortunately, after we moved into our new home, the farmer who'd been cutting the tall grass became ill and died before we could even meet him. Donald stepped up, as he does, bought a riding mower, and mowed the acreage himself. It's become an annual ritual.

My husband is from Chicago yet has longstanding connections to this area; both his parents were born in Seattle, and they sometimes took Donald and his twin brother to western Washington to visit relatives. Just as I'm finding good friends in the

Pacific Northwest, my husband is also finding his tribe. Donald plays guitar with musical people at least once a week. His musician friends are not only as devoted to Irish tunes as he is, but they also genuinely appreciate each other, even having potluck meals together. When I join them for a meal, I feel welcome and included.

In spring 2021, Donald was ready to commit to Whidbey Island and sell the Illinois property. Houses were in demand and ours was snapped up before it was even officially on the market. Soon a truckload of furniture, kitchenware, and books from the sold house arrived to be incorporated into our new home—and a new phase of our lives.

We live together full-time, contented if not always blissful. In our case, it's true that opposites attract; our tastes, habits, and priorities often conflict. The entry on "marriage" in our 2002 edition of *World Book Encyclopedia* states that "if a man and woman are of a different age, nationality, religion, or background, their chances of a successful marriage drop significantly." Though Donald and I both practice Buddhism, we have the odds against us because I am a European American six years younger than my Japanese American husband, among other issues. I suspect that even our brains are wired differently.

Biological anthropologist Helen Fisher observed in her book, *Anatomy of Love: A Natural History of Mating, Marriage, and Why We Stray*, that partners in a couple are "like two feet. They need each other to get ahead." Her studies of couples in China and the United States revealed that the three traits most associated with happy partnerships are empathy, emotional self-control, and focusing on the positive (what you like about your spouse). This gives me hope for marital success because anyone can develop those capacities. And Fisher stressed the importance of laughter. Humor helps put our problems in perspective.

As wry newspaper columnist Erma Bombeck used to say, "When humor goes, there goes civilization."

When our daughters went to college out-of-state and then took jobs even farther away, Donald and I figured we'd be forever traveling to visit them and their families. Yet, here we are, marveling at their regular presence in our lives, chatting and laughing with each other during Sunday suppers. Sunday is the day Emily and Alex are free. Besides tending to their farm, they run a deli business in Greenbank, a community in the middle of Whidbey Island. Stephanie and John, having left New York City, are settled in their Whidbey home with their cat and a new baby.

When I take care of our grandchild, Miro, my heart does a little jig, rejoicing that I get to be a grandmother. *I'm still here! So glad to get to know you, little one.* At naptime, I play soft music and walk around and around our kitchen island with Miro till he falls asleep. He always settles on my left. Maybe he prefers that side so he can hear my heartbeat. Or is it because of the padding on the left side? The right side is skin and bones.

I rarely wear my prosthetic right breast. If somebody notices my post-mastectomy appearance and has a second look, so be it. At sixty-three years of age, it's not as much of an issue for me as it is for some women. My husband and I are fine with my reconfigured body. It doesn't really concern anyone else, except maybe Miro.

I'd told Stephanie I wanted a cushiony chest on which to hold my grandchildren, if I ever had any. That was a factor in my decision for a single mastectomy rather than a double. Two years later, she was pregnant with Miro, and here I am with a soft place for the baby to fall asleep. In a configuration of love, he and I circle around the island at the pace of the CD's harp strings. I can feel Miro's body relax into slumber on my shoulder and, in that moment, all is right with the world.

Epilogue

....

STAR BIRTH—FARE WELL

To bring oneself to others makes the whole planet less lonely.
The nobility of everybody trying boggles the mind.

—MARY KARR

I attended Healing Circles in Langley, Washington, for three years after I was diagnosed with breast cancer. Our cancer circle met twice a month, giving me a place to be real and to heal. Due to the COVID-19 pandemic, Healing Circles went online and consequently, global. Diana Lindsay started training circle hosts in sixteen countries to meet the demand.

During a training when I was assisting Diana, we did a check-in with participants as to how they were feeling. A woman from California said she felt she'd been dragged under the waves once too often and was having trouble keeping her head above water, both financially and emotionally.

"Will the highs ever be as high as the lows are low?" she asked.

Her concerns got me thinking. There were many reasons to feel depressed and anxious during such unexpected times. The lows felt very low indeed. Yet is it our goal to always be riding a wave, on a high of happiness? I remember how, when one of my mentors told an ancient story, she would ask, "What may we learn from this?" Her question inspired a broad perspective. Whatever we experience, whether pleasant or painful, is part of our education on Earth. As with nutrition, I don't just eat desserts all day, sweet as they may be. I choose what nourishes me in the long run and allows me to grow.

In a similar way, suffering can help me grow, as it carves out space in my heart for more compassion. I'm not always in a place of light and peace. My friend sent me a moving essay she'd written about her aunt. Then she sent me a note, regretting it. She worried I'd be troubled by the account of her aunt's grueling cancer treatments. Yes, the story evoked emotions, and yes, it reminded me of how chemotherapy affected me when I had treatment. But I assured my friend she need not hold back in sharing such things. These stories are about my people. They are where I find fellowship with those who know what I've been through. It is not a morbid interest; it is a kinship. We're all struggling with something.

I've read that the densest clumps of matter in the Eagle Nebula become stars. The cloudy bits become bright shedding light that will reach the Earth in a millennium or so. I'm learning through the days and nights, highs and lows, so all have value to me. The black pumice stone of sorrow polishes my rough spots until I glow once again, softer this time, with ears to listen and tears for your pain.

When I'm feeling cloudy, I know it's time to call on my Better Self. Her resources are fresh air, loved ones, and prayers. Naps help too. I recharge both my super and subtle powers. How do I reactivate my hope muscle? Sometimes with quiet breath and sometimes with noisy dancing. And by visiting the trees.

Come with me! The morning star is up.

ACKNOWLEDGMENTS

Thank you, first and foremost, to my husband and our children and their families. You are the reason and context for my every breath.

Wolf Pack! Joan Prefontaine, Allison Wolf, and Jon Wolf, you had my back! You cheered me on with messages and flowers.

Thank you, lifelong friend, Amy Gunderson! You gave me comfort during treatments, texting messages for healing and rest, and arriving in person when I needed moral support.

Thank you to all my deep-thinking and compassionate friends in the Midwest as well as in the Pacific Northwest. So many bodhisattvas in my life! Yes, we did emerge from the Earth for a purpose.

Those involved with Healing Circles Langley, Healing Circles Global, and Commonweal have been at the core of my healing. I particularly want to thank Diana Lindsay, Susanne Fest, Michael Lerner, and Lynn and Jeff Nelsen. Though Kelly Lindsay is no longer with us, I wish to thank him as well.

I am grateful for the medical healers who helped me through my cancer journey. Also helpful were the people who created the ihadcancer.com website and those who have contributed to it.

I've been fortunate to write among creative people, particularly at Ragdale Artist Community and the Off Campus Writers Workshop, both in Illinois. I've also grown from writing workshops with Lynda Barry, Anne LeClair, Nancy Slonim Aronie, Rebecca Hill, Dorothy Randall Gray, Kate Stivers, Christina Baldwin, Ann Linnea, and Margaret Bendet.

Thank you, Joan Prefontaine, Mickey Silverstein, Jenny Goff, Joan Mage, Cece Otto, Janet Lombardi, Kathleen Lorden, and others who gave me feedback on my work or simply spurred me on by showing interest and enthusiasm. You kept me going!

Special thanks to writer and literary critic, David Mura, for helping me think more deeply about my mixed marriage, raising topics I will be addressing more fully in the future.

I benefitted from a meeting with Rick Castellano of Island County Historical Society, who clarified the history of the place I now live, before it was ever called Whidbey Island.

Thank you to Steve and Sharon Fiffer, who, along with my fellow Wesley writers, found my writing worth improving. Your immense patience and good humor buoyed me up along the way.

Word wizard, Annie Tucker, you were the wind in my sails as I finished my manuscript. What a great voyage we had!

About the Author

Photo credit: Michael Stadler

BARBARA WOLF TERAO is a writer, mother, and grandmother living on Whidbey Island in Washington. Born and raised in the Midwest, she's been a teacher, psychologist, land ethic leader, television host, newspaper columnist, book reviewer, and editor. Her articles and essays have appeared in *Orion, The Seattle Times, AHP Perspective, Realize, Art in the Time of Unbearable Crisis,* and *Cabin Life,* and on her Of the Earth website (ofthebluepla.net).

SELECTED TITLES FROM SHE WRITES PRESS

She Writes Press is an independent publishing company founded to serve women writers everywhere. Visit us at www.shewritespress.com.

Bless the Birds: Living with Love in a Time of Dying by Susan J. Tweit. $16.95, 978-1-64742-036-9. Writer Susan Tweit and her economist-turned-sculptor husband Richard Cabe had just settled into their version of a "good life" when Richard saw thousands of birds one day—harbingers of the brain cancer that would kill him two years later. This intimate memoir chronicles their journey into the end of his life, framed by their final trip together: a 4,000-mile, long-delayed honeymoon road trip.

Here We Grow: Mindfulness through Cancer and Beyond by Paige Davis. $16.95, 978-1-63152-381-6. At thirty-eight years old, after receiving a breast cancer diagnosis, Paige Davis ventures into an unlikely love affair of a lifetime—and embraces cancer through a lens of love rather than as a battle to be fought.

Falling Together: How to Find Balance, Joy, and Meaningful Change When Your Life Seems to be Falling Apart by Donna Cardillo. $16.95, 978-1-63152-077-8. A funny, big-hearted self-help memoir that tackles divorce, caregiving, burnout, major illness, fears, and low self-esteem—and explores the renewal that comes when we are able to meet these challenges with courage.

The Buddha at My Table: How I Found Peace in Betrayal and Divorce by Tammy Letherer. $16.95, 978-1-63152-425-7. On a Tuesday night, just before Christmas, after he had put their three children in bed, Tammy Letherer's husband shattered her world and destroyed every assumption she'd ever made about love, friendship, and faithfulness. In the aftermath of this betrayal, however, she finds unexpected blessings—and, ultimately, the path to freedom.

The Field House: A Writer's Life Lost and Found on an Island in Maine by Robin Clifford Wood. $16.95, 978-1-64742-045-1. When Robin Clifford Wood stepped onto the sagging floorboards of Rachel Field's long-neglected home on the rugged shores of an island in Maine fifty years after Field's death and began dredging up the brilliant but largely forgotten writer's history, the journey took her farther than she ever dreamed possible.